YOUR MONEY, DAY ONE

How to Start Right and End Rich

Michael J. Wagner, M.A. Ed.

BookSurge Publishing
Charleston, SC

Your Money, Day One: How to Start Right and End Rich

Copyright © 2009 by Michael J. Wagner

To order additional copies, please contact:

BookSurge Publishing
7290 B Investment Drive
Charleston, SC 29418
www.booksurge.com
1-866-308-6235

First Edition

ISBN 1-4392-2366-1

Library of Congress Control Number: 2008912098

Cover design by
Cory Grosser of Grosser Design and Strategy, Los Angeles, CA

Printed in the United States of America

To my Mother, Father and my sister Carol

CONTENTS

Contents

Contents

Contents

Contents

Contents

INTRODUCTION

Will you control your money or will your money control you?

Think back for a minute about how much *formal* training you have gotten in your life about how to handle money. I mean *real* training about key financial terms and strategies, concepts that establish a foundation for your financial future. My extensive experience with young adults today indicates to me they don't get much at all, if any. Not in school, not at home and they certainly don't seek it out as they spend countless hours on their computers. Recently I had an interesting conversation that really reinforced this point.

I was speaking with a young man, Rudy, about what he had been up to. Rudy is a senior at a Los Angeles public high school and he is only months away from graduating. He attends a year-round school system, and he was off track and on a break before finishing his last few weeks of school. I had not seen him in a while. He told me he found a job at Subway through a friend. I was thrilled, as I am a huge proponent of young adults working. He had been working for a couple of weeks, and I inquired as to whether he had yet been paid. He said, "yes, a couple of times." I asked him if he was saving any of his money. He looked at me and just laughed. He said, "No way, I just spend it all." I wasn't surprised by his answer, he is 17, the typical high school kid. Work, get paid and spend it. Why wouldn't he, based on how our consumer based society is set up; why should he do anything different?

I said, "Rudy do you have a bank account?" He said, "No." I said, "Rudy, you need to get a bank account." He said, "Do you mean like a savings account?" I said, "Yes, that is a bank account." He said, "Yeah, I have a savings account at Wells Fargo, but it doesn't have any money in it."

So I took the opportunity to help him understand some basics of what he could start doing to take control of his financial life. I explained that I was writing a book for young adults just like him. I expressed to him that he is at the opportune time to begin and asked if he had a few more minutes so I could show him something. I pulled out a chart that I share with kids showing the power of compound interest, similar to the one in chapter 11. I explained the concept of compound interest and the variety of possibilities that exist at different ages and different rates of return. He listened quietly and looked at me and said, "I don't know how the interest rate thing works." I looked at him and said, "It is the rate of return for a mutual fund." He replied, "I don't know what a mutual fund is." I said to him, "You don't know what a mutual fund is or how it works?" He looked at me and shook his head. I said, "Rudy, I can help you."

Rudy is not alone in his lack of understanding of simple financial concepts, and how to develop sound habits. As basic as the conversation was between us I knew one thing for sure, after Rudy saw the information he was intrigued. I thought to myself, if he was able to obtain the concept of compound interest and the power it holds when combined with time after our brief conversation, just think what he could learn if he took the time to understand the importance of establishing savings habits and to begin developing sound money management skills. From our conversation, he already knew that he could control his financial situation, he just didn't know how or where to start. Rudy reminded me why I have taken up this cause. YOUR MONEY, DAY ONE is designed to assist the millions of young adults just like Rudy and you.

How common do you think it is today for young adults, like yourself, to take money and blow it, to just go out and spend it on anything and everything possible? Do you know someone like this? Are you like that? Have you ever given it much thought to what you would do if you need money and didn't have it? Hey, let me guess, you're just going to charge it. Here's a fact on how effective that method has become. It is common for a person today to have, on average, over $9,000 in credit card debt on four or more credit cards. Ask yourself, do you really think that is an effective money management system? Believe it or not, it is more common than you may think because people have formed bad habits and have lost control.

In a recent survey, high school students openly voiced that they wish they would learn more about money while in school. They also wish they would learn more about money from their parents. Parents are asking the schools to teach their children more about money. The schools assume the responsibility should rest on the shoulders of the parents. It's a viscous circle. While all of the finger pointing is going on there is one person who is stuck in the middle and becomes the victim – YOU. Schools are not applying the necessary resources to teach young adults how to effectively manage money. Today's parents are busier than ever with everyday life and trying to make ends meet. Further, many have not learned and/or practiced the best financial decisions to set the example or impart the wisdom to their children. So, how are you supposed to develop the necessary habits and skills needed to establish a successful financial future? The answer lies within you. You need to take control of this portion of your life now.

This book is about you taking control of your money. It is about you starting early in your life, right now, making decisions that will affect your life. It is about dispelling the negative connotation that 'budgeting' is a life restricting activity that means you can't have fun. It is about learning to 'live within your means.' It is about you making the right choices and sometimes even sacrifices that will benefit you in your life now and in the future. This book is for YOU.

The way you begin is doing what you are right now, taking the initiative to establish sound financial habits that will provide the foundation needed for a successful financial future. There is no 'untold secret' that holds the key to becoming rich. It is about establishing a certain lifestyle, no different than making decisions about eating right or exercising. Learning now will enable you to take advantage of the two key elements to a successful financial future and that is – time and compound interest. When you break it down in its simplest form, the longer you have your money earning interest the more you will have, period. It is that simple. You don't have to have a high paying job; you don't have to come from a rich family; you don't need to be an entrepreneurial genius. You can begin even before you get a job. Think about all those times you receive money like holidays, confirmations, bar mitzvahs, and birthdays. You have access to money, you just don't really think about it, plus you don't know what to do with it.

How much money can you acquire? Let's look at an example. You are 16 years old and begin working. You start saving $100 a month in a mutual fund, which averages 8% return. At age 62, after saving for about 47 years, you would have over $626,000, all by investing less than $57,000. While this may not be enough money to retire 47 years from now just think - if this can be done with a mere $100 a month starting at age 16, what could be done by saving even more money as time progresses, your income increases and you become financially savvy?

YOUR MONEY, DAY ONE provides you with a comprehensive and easy to understand how-to guide to practice successful financial habit building. Remember, the one advantage that you possess is – time. The quicker you understand and incorporate certain habits and strategies, the sooner it will help you realize and achieve your goals, probably years, even decades ahead of your peers. The one question to continually ask is, "Will you control your money or will your money control you?" As a young adult, you may not yet have control over many aspects of your life, but you can have control over this. There is no better time than the present, to take control.

Let's get back to our friend Rudy for a moment. Clearly, Rudy had not been taught about handling personal finances either in school or by his parents, yet he was eager to learn. When we talked about starting to save, I asked him if he thought he could put away $50 per paycheck. Rudy thought he could do that easily and maybe even a little more. We talked about how he could save money in his savings account and when he had gathered enough he could take that money after his 18th birthday and open an IRA mutual fund in his own name.

About six weeks after we spoke, just before graduation, Rudy, a high school senior from a working class family, employed at Subway part-time, came to see me again at my after-school program with some great news. In that short amount of time, Rudy had managed to save over $700 in his account. He explained to me that he was putting away $100 from each paycheck and if he had money left over on the next pay day, he was transferring it to the account as well. Rudy had already begun establishing a habit. He was feeling the thrill of having control of his money and seeing the money grow more quickly than he had ever imagined. We agreed that when he turns 18, I would personally escort him to open a mutual fund at a local discount brokerage firm. If Rudy can do it, so can you, even if you don't have a job. Let's get started and I'll show you how.

Chapter 1

EASY COME, EASY GO

Each day you will deal with decisions that will affect your personal finances. Understanding this information will give you a leg up on your peers in establishing a solid financial beginning and future. Let's get started with the specific information. Knowing how money will come to you is the first step in developing personal money management skills. Let's look at the different ways that money can come into your life.

Easy Money

The first way, and the easiest, *easy money* is money handed to you from your parents, such as an allowance. I have always teased children that parents are like **human ATM machines** and you don't even need an ATM card to receive the money.

Gifted Money

Another way you can get money is from specific **important events**

in your life, like birthdays and holidays and personal achievements such as bar mitzvahs, bat mitzvahs, confirmations, graduations and good grades. *Gifted money* can also be from an inheritance. This is when someone close to you passes away and you receive part of their estate (things they own, including money) that they leave behind. Most likely this would be from a grandfather or grandmother.

Earned Money

You can create your own entrepreneurial business opportunities by mowing lawns, delivering newspapers, babysitting, dog-walking, home chores or operating a stand selling drinks, to name a few. This may be your first experience with *earned money* before getting a job. When you are of legal age to obtain work, **the most common way to earn money is from a job** with a business at which you are considered an employee. Wages are paid either on an hourly rate or by a weekly or monthly salary.

Refund Money

Another way to obtain money is from **tax refunds generated from your wages**. This is the money that is taken from your paycheck, each time you are paid and kept by the selected government agencies. (We will address filing a tax return, in more detail, in a future section, along with how this money, that you have lived without, can make a difference in your financial future.) Depending on your individual tax situation, you may be eligible for tax *refund money*.

Three Ways to Use Money

Now that we have established the various ways you can obtain money we will look at the three ways of using your money. They are:

Spend it: always the crowd favorite, I have never met anyone who actually admitted they didn't like to.

Save it: letting your money earn money for future use, making money while you sleep.

Give it: donate to a charity or gift it in a meaningful way.

Spend It

Spending your money is not something that needs any explanation because everyone has experience and has mastered that activity. We will address budgeting later in the program which will allow you to accurately determine the amount of money that you will have available to spend on a regular basis.

Save It

The second way of using your money is to save it. We will spend a considerable amount of time on this subject as it is **one of the most important life skills** in planning for your financial future. For some people this is not a popular topic since we get so much gratification when we spend our money and accumulate so much stuff. The only problem is that as the years pass by, it is like snapping your fingers – before you know it, whoosh – you will lose one of the most precious resources you have – time. Once it passes it cannot be regained. To be able to successfully plan and build your financial future you have to take advantage of time and by doing so you will separate yourself from others around you.

Learn and practice this very simple concept, it will reward you and you will be admired. (Later in this program we will discuss in greater detail what I call The BIG 3, three financial strategies that will set you on this path.) As much gratification as you get from the act of spending your money, you will get the same, if not more, from taking the initiative to also save money.

Give It

The third and final way of using your money is by giving it away, or **giving back to the community** in which you live, specifically to the causes that you deem as valuable and important to you. When you take it upon yourself to help those who are less fortunate, that kindness and generosity will come back to you in a variety of positive ways, but most rewarding is the feeling you will experience in your heart by helping your fellow man. Always remember, as much as we try to insure that our lives go as planned, you may find yourself in an unfortunate life situation, whatever it may be, in which you may be on the receiving end of those same causes that you believed in and supported.

As much gratification as you get from the act of spending your money or saving your money, your greatest satisfaction may come from watching the money you give to the causes of your choice produce positive outcomes. It is more than the act of giving the money; it is truly demonstrating the type of human being you are to those around you. Let's get into the next part of the program.

Chapter 2

FOUR LETTER WORDS

I hope that when you saw the title of this section you didn't think that I was going to review all the bad four letter words that are used or, even worse, give you some new ones. I don't think your parents would be very happy about me doing that. I have been around plenty of kids and for that matter – adults too, and I have become very familiar with the use of 'four' letter words. It is really funny now-a-days how sometimes you will hear parents speaking around their kids and then when it comes to that 'four letter' expletive they try to delicately skate around it, they will mouth it without sound or spell it out the old fashion way. I always think "come on, like they don't know the word already?" or "like they haven't used it?" What we are going to address, however are some four letter words that are very important in developing valuable and worthwhile personal money management skills. These are words that your parents will definitely approve of and want you to know and use.

Cash

The first one that I always put at the top of my list, and I hope that you will put it on the top of yours is the word *cash*. (I can tell you that it is definitely on the top of my wife's list because she ALWAYS has it, ALWAYS!) CASH is one of the most beautiful and important four letter words in any language. **CASH has many advantages**, and some disadvantages as well. The one huge benefit of using and maintaining cash is that it provides you instant access to your money, which enables you to purchase goods and services without any further follow up on your part. The purchase doesn't get recorded on your bank statement from your bank; it doesn't get recorded by your credit card company, and you don't have to pay in the future for something you have purchased. Once you pay for the product or service, you will get a receipt and that's it. Finished!! Completed sale!!

That is the basic advantage, however, more than that, it is about taking responsibility for your personal financial situation. It is about developing a very important financial habit called budgeting. (We will discuss budgeting in more detail later.) The reason that **CASH is an effective budgeting tool** is that when you effectively use CASH you are in turn, limiting the amount of money that you spend. Let's look at a real life example. Let's say, for instance, that you walk into your favorite fast food restaurant, you have cash in your pocket and your friend has a credit card. One thing about carrying cash and using cash is that you automatically control or budget your money because you are consciously thinking about what else you may want or need to use your money for. You order the #3 meal that is less than $6. But your friend, because he is not carrying cash, doesn't consider the cost because it is going on 'plastic.' So, he orders the #3 meal, super sizes it, and for good measure throws in a chocolate shake and ends up spending around $10. A couple of things happen here. You get your change back and a receipt and your transaction is complete. But your friend, who has spent more money, has acquired debt for a fast food meal. Later, if he does not pay his credit card bill in full upon receipt, he will now pay interest on that $10 fast food meal meaning that he is actually paying more than $10. If he continues to do this it can add up quickly.

Why would you want to do that? That is a question that a lot of people never ask themselves. This example is a very true representation of the real world, evidenced by statistics supplied by CreditCard.com. U.S. consumers racked up an estimated $51 billion worth of fast food on their personal credit and debit cards in 2006, compared to $33.2 billion the year before. In addition to that, the average ticket for Visa purchases is consistently more than cash purchases.[1] By using CASH, you actually have paid the exact price of the meal, you have not acquired debt, and you are budgeting your money (not to mention actually eating healthier because you don't order more food).

Sure, people could say that when you run out of CASH you can just get more out of an ***ATM (automated teller machine)***. But if you take developing personal money management skills seriously, (which I believe you are or you wouldn't be reading this right now, unless your parents are forcing you) you will understand that having to constantly get money out of an ATM is kind of a hassle, and you will take notice, asking yourself why you are doing it so often.

Critics will say that it is risky to carry CASH because once you lose it, it cannot be replaced. This is about being responsible. I cannot remember the last time I lost CASH or my wallet. I am not saying that you should be walking around with a canvas bag that has a big dollar sign on it like you see in a cartoon, but you should carry an appropriate amount of cash in your wallet, purse or pocket for everyday spending. What I want you to get out of this very important four letter word, CASH, is that it plays an important part in your life and it can help you be very savvy with your money. As they say, "if you don't have the CASH, don't buy it!"

Bank

It shouldn't surprise you that I would choose the next four letter word considering that for the majority of my working life I was in the financial services industry working with and around money. Let's discuss

---

1 http://www.creditcards.com/statistics/credit-card-industry-facts-and-personal-debt-statistics.php

the word *bank*. **A BANK serves a very important and useful purpose** in the world. Banks have been around for a long time. The Bank of the Manhattan Company received its original charter to operate in 1799. Today there are thousands of banks. They all serve one purpose, to provide financial products and services to us, the general public. A bank is a place for us to **maintain our money in a safe place** while at the same time help make it grow by earning interest. Banks also provide products that assist us in achieving our financial goals and dreams, personal or business. For a young adult, a bank is a **great place to begin developing your personal money management skills**. Because of rules and regulations, banks will restrict you if you are under the age of 18 from opening a bank account on your own. However, you can ask your parents to accompany you to a bank and help you open an account so that you can establish yourself financially. This will give you firsthand experience with bank professionals. They will help you determine the type of account that will work for you. Most accounts will have access with a debit or ATM card. With the creation of the internet, you are able to open an account online, if you are 18 or older. But if you are just establishing your first accounts, taking the time to do it in person will allow you to ask questions and will provide a valuable life experience. This will take some initiative and responsibility, but the benefits of doing so will be worth it.

There are two basic types of accounts, a checking account and a savings account. A *checking account* will 'hold' your money that you deposit in it. The funds in the account are normally withdrawn by either writing a check or by using your debit card. With a checking account you will receive a monthly bank statement that will provide a history of the month's activity in the account for you to verify. That is why you save your receipts and log your activity in a transaction register. THIS IS A VERY IMPORTANT FUNCTION OF HAVING AN ACCOUNT. A *savings account* will also 'hold' your money that you deposit. To access your funds you must use a debit card, transfer it to your checking account, or physically go to the bank and use a savings withdrawal slip. While a savings account can be accessed by you, it is not typically a means to pay others. All savings accounts will be interest bearing – the bank or institution will pay you a preset rate of *interest* for maintaining your balance with them, only a certain few checking accounts offer the same feature, usually with a minimum balance requirement. The types of accounts offered vary from bank to bank, so you need to speak to a bank professional for more details or research them on the bank's website.

Banks favor loyal customers, so starting an account with a bank early in your life can be advantageous. After you complete the account opening procedure you will receive a small packet of information, a **series of brochures called account disclosures**. These are required by the government to explain, in detail, everything you need to know about the account(s) that you open. I would strongly encourage you to read them and get into the habit of reading important documents like this, because it will give you a clear understanding of exactly what you can and cannot do and also what the BANK can and cannot do. Plus, as you move forward in your life **it will be critical that you read and understand everything you sign**.

The financial experience you gain by opening a bank account will reward you in so many ways. For example, reading a monthly or quarterly bank statement will explain to you the activity that has taken place. Regardless if it is a checking or savings account, you will have to **learn how to balance your account on a monthly basis**. This means that all the money you believe you have matches what the bank says you have. As you can imagine, when the amounts do not match you have a problem. Believe it or not, there are a lot of people who never do this and even more that don't know how. Being a branch manager for many years I used to witness it firsthand when customers would come into the bank with a problem and I would ask them, "When is the last time you balanced your account?" They would get a blank look on their faces and shrug their shoulders. When this happens it is really hard to try to help someone because you have no idea when the problem occurred. Please, don't develop this habit, take the time each month to balance your bank account. With the variety of software programs available like Quicken or Microsoft Money the process of balancing your accounts can be simplified. It is your responsibility to manage your accounts properly, after all it is your hard earned money – take care of it.

Since we are on the subject of the word BANK, I feel it is appropriate to address some closely related topics.

Federal Deposit Insurance Corporation (FDIC)

The Federal Deposit Insurance Corporation is a federal government organization originally formed in 1933, that **provides deposit insurance to individuals** who have money in checking, savings and other deposit accounts (including *certificates of deposit (CDs)*). This agency was formed after the Great Depression in the United States (after many Americans lost everything as a result of bank closures) as a method to provide stability to the U.S. economy and ease the fears of depositors. Deposit insurance gives depositors the security that their money, when combined and deposited, into banks is insured, up to $100,000 or more. This means that if there is some unforeseen circumstance or negative business conditions that force a bank to close, the customers (depositors) will not lose their money. It should be noted that since the origination of the FDIC in 1934, no depositor has lost any money as a result of a bank failure.

The insurance limit is good for total deposits *per bank* in which accounts are held. It should be understood that FDIC insurance *only* applies to deposits. Policies and procedures outlining the variety of accounts, the manner in which they are established and how they are affected can be addressed with a customer service representative or by reviewing information on the FDIC website.

Insurance coverage by the **FDIC does not apply to securities, mutual funds or other investments** banks may offer. To learn more about FDIC insurance visit their website www.fdic.gov.

Credit Union

When you are deciding where to establish your banking accounts there will be another financial organization you will come across called a credit union. A **credit union**, as defined by InvestorWords.com is "a non-profit financial institution that is owned and operated entirely by its members."[2] Credit unions also **offer financial products and services to 'members'** including checking or share draft accounts, savings accounts and loans.

To conduct business with a credit union you have to be a member. Once you establish an account and become a member you are considered to have partial ownership in the credit union. Normally to join a credit union a person must be affiliated with or belong to a specific organization or company. This includes companies, professional memberships, community organizations and more.

Credit unions are set up as not-for-profit cooperatives that are owned by members (depositors) and are managed and governed typically by a volunteer board of directors. As members join credit unions they pool their assets together in order to provide loans and other financial products and services to each other. By doing so, it allows credit unions to be able to pay dividends to their members in the form of increased savings rates, lower loan rates and reduced service fees. (This is a good opportunity to ask your parents if they belong to a credit union which might offer better rates of interest and more attractive products and services). Similar to that of FDIC, federal credit unions also have what is called the **National Credit Union Share Insurance Fund (NCUSIF)**. This federal government agency charters and supervises federal credit unions. The NCUSIF provides insurance, up to $100,000, for their deposits and **protects members from suffering losses if a federally insured credit union would go out of business**. As with the FDIC, no individual member of an NCUSIF federally insured credit union has ever lost money. Policies and procedures outlining the variety of accounts, the manner in which they are established and how they are affected when it comes to insurance coverage can be addressed with a customer service representative or by reviewing information on the NCUA website. Insurance coverage by the NCUSIF, as with the FDIC, **does not apply to securities, mutual funds**

2 http://www.investorwords.com/1214/credit_union.html

or other investments credit unions may offer. To learn more about NCUSIF insurance visit their website www.ncua.gov.

Card

It is only appropriate, I think, since we are on the subject of the importance of the word – BANK – that we would continue on with other four letter words that are related to that word. The next four letter word is the word CARD. This is a general word and the uses of the word CARD are many. It is used in a variety of personal, business and financial applications. When it is combined with two other financial terms, CARD becomes a very common way of using money in your life and developing your personal money management skills.

Debit Card

The first word we will combine with CARD is DEBIT. According to InvestorDictionary.com, the definition for the word DEBIT is "a charge to a customer's access account (savings account) or deposit account (checking account)."[3] When you DEBIT your account you are subtracting money from your account or decreasing the funds you have available. A *debit card*, according to InvestorDictionary.com, is a plastic card that **allows individuals to gain immediate access to money** in a checking or savings account through the use of electronic fund transfer systems via ATMs or the EFT point-of-sale system.[4] A DEBIT CARD is often referred to as an ATM card. To clarify, ATM is short for Automated Teller Machine or machines from which you obtain money with your DEBIT CARD. **EFT is short for Electronic Funds Transfer**, also referred to as a point of sale system. These are electronic machines at a business that communicate electronically with a financial institution to obtain the approval for a specific purchase or sale of goods.

While we are discussing an ATM and DEBIT CARD, this is a good time to briefly discuss the actual physical machine called an ATM. The

3 http://www.investordictionary.com/dictionary/terms/c.aspx
4 http://www.investordictionary.com/dictionary/terms/c.aspx

ATM was developed to provide people with 24 hour access to their money in a convenient manner. When you open your bank account(s) you will be given a DEBIT CARD for withdrawing money from the ATM. When you are opening your accounts the bank professional will ask you to select a PIN number, which stands for Personal Identification Number. After you insert your card into the ATM, it will ask for your PIN number and it will direct you through the necessary steps for you to receive the money you request or other transactions available. **NEVER WALK AWAY FROM THE ATM MACHINE WITHOUT TAKING YOUR CARD OUT OF THE MACHINE**. It will remind you, that is the beeping sound you hear while you are standing there.

Credit Card

I referenced earlier the combination of the words DEBIT and CARD to explain an important financial term. There is another combination of words that emphasizes even a greater financial term and one that almost everyone is familiar with in some form or fashion, the term CREDIT CARD. I know, I can see your face right now, you are rolling your eyes and thinking, "c'mon you've got to be kidding me, you're going to talk about what a CREDIT CARD is, who doesn't know what a CREDIT CARD is?" Keep in mind that my goal is not to bore you, but to provide valuable and necessary information on financial terms, while at the same time help you to develop sound personal money management skills. According to InvestorDictionary.com, the definition of CREDIT refers to money loaned or the ability of an individual or company to borrow money. It is a charge to a customer's account.[5] A *credit card* is a plastic card with a magnetic strip, issued by a bank or business that allows the holder to purchase goods and services on credit and pay for them at a later time, usually with interest.[6] A CREDIT CARD can also be referred to as a charge card, which is a term used in the retail sector, like large department store chains. When you use a CREDIT CARD, **you are borrowing or being lent money to enable**

---

5 http://www.investordictionary.com/dictionary/terms/c.aspx
6 http://www.creditcards.com/statistics/credit-card-industry-facts-and-personal-debt-statistics.php

you to purchase a product or service. By doing so, you are in the act of CREDITing your account or simply adding money to the balance of your CREDIT CARD account.

CREDIT CARDs and DEBIT CARDs are two of the largest financial product developments. The creation of these products has had an incredible impact on how we as a society are able to handle money without having to physically carry it around with us. Here are some general facts about CREDIT CARDS supplied by CreditCards.com: [7]

- Consumers carry more than 1 billion Visa cards worldwide— more than 450 million of those cards are in the United States. (Source: Visa USA)
- U.S. Visa cardholders alone conduct more than $1 trillion in annual volume. That's $1,000,000,000,000. (Source: Visa USA)
- Total U.S. consumer debt (not including home mortgage debt) reached $2.46 trillion in June 2007, an increase of $70 billion, up from $2.39 trillion at the end of 2006. (Source: Federal Reserve)
- Nearly one in every three consumer purchases in the United States is made with a payment card—including credit, debit, and prepaid products. (Source: Visa USA)
- Of every $100 spent by consumers, nearly $40 is in a form other than cash or check. (Source: Visa USA)

These facts give you an idea of not just the shear volume, dollars and cents of the CREDIT CARD industry, but how revolutionary this financial product has become and what an impact it has had on our way of life as consumers.

Fees

Continuing with other four letter words that are associated with the word BANK, one that draws an unbelievable amount of criticism and is

---

7 http://www.creditcards.com/statistics/credit-card-industry-facts-and-personal-debt-statistics.php

a central source of frustration for the general public, is the word *fees*. This is a word that will become all too familiar in your life. There is always pressure on the financial services industry and businesses to look for new and innovative ways to increase bottom line profits, in addition to increasing prices and sales of products and services. According to InvestorDictionary.com the definition of the word FEES is "remuneration for a service performed or for a privilege."[8] Remuneration is **a sum of money or a charge for having some type of service provided**. For instance, when you attend a movie you will be charged an admission fee to attend. The service the theater provides is showing you the movie in exchange for the admission fee. In the financial world FEES are assessed for banking services. These FEES can be for such things as printing and providing an account statement, which may cost anywhere from $5 to $10 depending on the type of account you maintain. Other FEES may include an ATM fee, assessed anywhere from $2 to $5 to access your money from another bank's ATM. As a rule of thumb, DO NOT use another financial institution's ATM unless you absolutely must. In this instance there may be double FEES incurred because you may be assessed a fee by both the financial institution you are using to obtain the money and by your own BANK. For example, let's say you and your friends are out and you forget to get some CASH before they pick you up. You ask them to stop at ABC BANK (not your bank) and you use the ATM to get $20. Before the ATM dispenses the money it advises you of the fee being assessed, let's say it is $2. But on the other end of the transaction your BANK also charges you for using a competitor's ATM and it assesses you a similar fee of $2. So, for withdrawing $20, from a competitor's ATM, you have been assessed a total of $4 in FEES. Well, if you do the simple math that means you paid 20% in FEES. You might say, "Big deal." But what it really means is that after you pay the FEES you really only have $16 left to spend. Ask yourself, what did you receive for the $4 that you paid? Only convenience. BARRING SOME UNFORESEEN CIRCUMSTANCE do not pay unnecessary FEES.

8 http://www.investordictionary.com/dictionary/terms/c.aspx

Remember that after you open your BANK account you will be given a packet of disclosure forms. This will include all the information you need to know about the FEES that you may be assessed. You can also ask the banking representative at the time you are opening your account to **go over the most common FEES that will be associated with your account**.

Before we move on, I would like to make a general recommendation regarding FEES. When you notice that there are FEES being assessed, it is totally acceptable to inquire as to what the FEE(S) are and why they are being assessed. It is also good business to ask if the FEE(S) can be waived, I always figure there are two possible answers – either yes or no. If the FEE(S) can be waived, that is more money in your pocket. There are times when the person you are speaking with will not have the power to waive the FEE(S) or the FEE(S) will not be able to be waived, but hey, at least you asked. When you do it, always be kind and polite; remember the old adage, "you will attract more bees with honey, than you will with vinegar." (Don't ask me who came up with that – I have no idea. I just know I have heard it hundreds of times and by the way, I have never tried it and I wouldn't suggest you should either – it could be dangerous, especially if you are allergic to bee stings.)

I know you are probably thinking that this is not what you thought it was going to be when you initially saw the title of this section, 'Four Letter Words.' I am sorry to disappoint you but I hope that the information so far has been both informative and helpful. I have a few more four letter words to share but I am not going to go into as much detail as I have with the prior words. Don't take it wrong, it isn't that I think they are less important, but we will be covering them in greater detail later when they will be more relevant and will make more sense.

Save

The next four letter word is *save*. This word can have a variety of meanings but the easiest way to explain it for this purpose **is putting money aside, spending less money** or not throwing money away. Putting money aside means that you don't spend all your money when you have it available. To save is to spend less. I revert back to the story of the difference of using CASH versus the CREDIT CARD at the restaurant. By using CASH you were able to SAVE by spending less money. There is an old saying that you may have heard by now that when you spend money on something that you (or your parents) may not feel is a worthwhile purchase it is said that you are 'throwing your money away,' or you have wasted it. It doesn't actually mean taking your money and throwing it in the trash, though I guess this could happen in a sense if you don't like what you bought or it was of poor quality and you end up throwing it away. I am sure right now you can think of an instance in which this happened to you.

Debt

One thing that happens, more often than not, is that if you do not develop effective personal money management skills at an early age with a specific emphasis on the ability to SAVE, then you are left with no choice but to resort to other financial means to purchase products and services, usually by using credit or borrowing money that you don't have. By using credit, you will increase your chances of acquiring DEBT. When you become in *debt*, **meaning you now owe money to someone**, be it a family member, friends, bank, finance company, etc., this will significantly decrease your ability to SAVE. You will now have to begin paying it back to those who helped you out. This may significantly interfere with your ability to SAVE, because you are repaying debt that probably could have been avoided in the first place. Don't take it the wrong way, I am not totally against debt or credit cards, but rather favor you successfully managing your debt while developing sound money management skills.

Zero

There is not a more appropriate time to discuss this next word than right now. Especially when we just finished discussing the word DEBT. The word is *zero*. There are multiple ways to apply this word in your financial life. The word ZERO can provide a feeling of exhilaration and happiness or a feeling of sadness, depression, anxiety and panic. When you hear those two ways of feeling, which seems more inviting? I hope you will say the first one, since that is the feeling you will have in your life when you strive and maintain mostly ZERO DEBT. You'll notice that I say "mostly" because there are going to be times in your life, like everyone's, when you will have DEBT. It may be from loans that you obtained for attending college, or a new car, a house, etc. The other feelings that are associated with the word ZERO, sadness, depression, anxiety and panic reflect not being able to SAVE your money and manage it in an appropriate manner. Your bank account reflects it when the balance says – ZERO. You do not want to get yourself into this position which is why we explore the double meaning and feelings associated with the word ZERO. Remember them; they will go a long way in your life.

Time

That brings us to another four letter word, TIME. It is one of the most important tools that you have on your side right now. As we will discuss later in greater detail, the addition of *time* when combined with other financial ingredients is one of the most successful money management recipes there is. The explanation is simple. The longer you have for your money to earn interest (which is the money someone is willing to pay you for letting them hold it and use it) and for it to earn interest on the interest, which is called compounding interest, the greater your savings will be. The key element that will make it grow in size is the length of TIME. Bottom line, **the longer the period of TIME, the greater chance you will have to build a successful financial life for yourself**.

I don't want to sound like your parents or that I am trying to lecture you, because that is the farthest thing from what I am trying to do, but it will amaze you just how fast TIME will go by in your life. So when you sit back and think oh, I have plenty of TIME, before you know it the real world begins to take over and TIME will move at light speed. Take advantage of this, you are not an *old person* like your parents. Be young and smart, do it differently than them and really show them that young people are better today. This might be one of those times that you can say, "Move over; let me handle this!" **Develop a friendship with TIME early on and it will be one of the best friends you will ever have**.

Free

Lastly, there is a four letter word that almost everyone loves. It is also one of those words with a double meaning. The word I am referring to is *free*. When we hear or see the word FREE our brains are programmed to feel excitement and to respond with the word 'yes.' It can also give us a sense of relief and a feeling of contentment.

It goes something like this. You are greeted by someone, usually with a clipboard or an index card and pen in hand and they will say, "Would you like to receive a free t-shirt?" (Or whatever they are giving away. You will see this in full force at college – it will happen all the time). This is called the 'hook,' a free gift that they will give you if you complete a form or entry for a product or service. However by doing so, you have just given them all of your personal information. They will enter it into their company database and can now begin contacting you and marketing all kinds of products and services. I have never received anything worthwhile by subjecting myself to this kind of activity and I would strongly urge you to avoid it. If someone wants to do business with you and they need your personal information, do it in a professional work environment. You don't need to be discussing your personal information, for all to hear, at a booth, a street fair, or a retail counter. **From this four letter word FREE, take this away: if it sounds too good to be true it normally is. Whenever you hear the word FREE, it means: PROCEED WITH CAUTION!**

The word FREE can also give you a sense of relief and contentment. You can feel FREE from restrictions that strain your financial situation if you are not in debt or overextended. Placing yourself in a precarious financial position becomes a constant struggle. Being DEBT FREE and not living with this uncomfortable situation provides opportunities in life that will make it more rewarding. Developing successful money management skills will give you that feeling of being FREE, but in a different and more enjoyable sense.

Well, we've done it. We have discussed four letter words and hopefully you have learned how to use them in a way in which you will never have to mouth them or spell them because you are afraid someone may hear you and be offended by their inappropriateness. Despite only having four letters, these words are important financial terms that will help you gain financial management skills that you can apply in your life forever. Great job sticking with it and now we just keep moving on.

Chapter 3

HEY! I GOT MY FIRST CHECK

One way of receiving money that we touched upon previously is having a job and earning wages. Even if you do not yet have a job, this is going to be the most common way you will receive money in your life, unless you have been graced with super nice parents that give you boatloads of money every month or you were bequeathed some unbelievable inheritance or if you are over 18 and won the lottery. If that is the case will you adopt me?

But seriously, **it is very important for you to be able to understand all the aspects of a *paycheck*** so that when you receive it you will have an idea of what each 'deduction' is and what it means. This is important, since it will be affecting your pay and ultimately the money on which you will be living. This may also be your first exposure to the financial terms – *gross pay* and *net pay* – and understanding the difference between them.

The Puzzled Store Clerk

While vacationing with my family in an upscale suburb of Chicago, we decided to stop by the local mall to shop. We entered a department store, found our way to the lower level and were walking by the customer service counter. I noticed a young man, around 20, who appeared to be relatively new to the job since his name was written on his name tag with a marker. When I walked by, I saw that he was holding a piece of paper that was the same size as a payroll check. Being discreet, I continued to observe him as he had a quizzical look upon his face, something between utter confusion and disbelief. He finally picked up the phone and called for a supervisor. I continued to shop. A woman approached and asked him what he needed. He said, "Where's all my money?" She looked at him and replied, "What do you mean?" He said, "This is not all my money." She requested to see the piece of paper, and now I knew it was his paycheck. He handed the piece of paper over to her and she said, "This is your paycheck for the hours that you worked, why?" He said, "But I should have more money than this." She said to him, "Well you worked so many hours and then you have to pay taxes." He said to her, "What do you mean I have to pay taxes, what for?" She said, "You have to pay taxes to the government." He looked at her with this wrinkled frown across his forehead and said, "For what?" At this point she looked at him in disbelief and just handed the check back to him and quietly walked away. She noticed that I had been watching the two of them interact, she smiled and had a look on her face like – you have got to be kidding me, he didn't know? I felt badly for the young man because it was apparent that he either never had a job before or at least did not have any previous work experience dealing with gross pay, net pay and deductions.

The store clerk stood there in total shock; his paycheck was obviously not what he thought it was going to be in dollars and cents. As I began to walk away with my wife, I said to her that he had probably already gone out and spent his paycheck and now the paycheck would not cover what he had already spent in cash or even worse, charged on his credit card. **It is a common but grave mistake when people spend money before they receive it or worse spend money they do not have. This habit is very dangerous and the consequences can be very harmful.**

I share this story because most likely this young man was told this information in an orientation meeting. This meeting is normally conducted after you are hired for a job by a representative from the human resource department who goes over a very large amount of information in a very short period of time. The new employee is excited and also nervous about getting started, all the information becomes a blur, he never goes back to review anything and then BAM! he is in this young man's position. I share this story because adults tend to make assumptions about what young people know. I know that I think about it all the time when I work with young adults. If they are doing something that they have never done before how are they supposed to know how to do it correctly? That is why training is so important for people to be able to complete an assignment correctly and, more important than that, to develop good habits. By understanding the basic information that is on your paycheck, you will not be surprised by the basic 'required' deductions that will appear.

Earnings Statement

Employers can provide a variety of earnings statements to their employees that will contain their paycheck and payroll information. Let's take a look at the *earnings statement*. When you look at it, it will have the following information on it in some form or fashion:

- Title of the document, e.g. Earnings Statement (a formal name for pay stub.)
- The official pay period, typically with a beginning date of the pay period, an ending date and also the date the check was issued.
- A logo of the actual entity that produces your check. (In today's world a lot of business functions are outsourced or performed by companies with a specific expertise like payroll, such as ADP.)
- The name and address of your employer.

- The filing status, either single or married, that you completed on a W-4 form provided to you when you were hired. The W-4 form is used by the Internal Revenue Service or IRS. (This is the Federal agency that oversees the collection of your federal taxes that will be withheld from your paycheck. We will be discussing this agency in greater detail in a later section.)
- The number of exemptions that you have claimed. The definition of exemption, according to the IRS Glossary of Terms, is: "the amount that taxpayers can claim for themselves, their spouses, and eligible dependents. There are two types of exemptions-personal and dependent. Each exemption reduces the amount of tax you will have withheld from your wages." [1]
- Your name and mailing address.
- Your social security number, but normally it will never display the entire number for security purposes. It may have the last four digits so you can verify that the paycheck is being reported under your name correctly.
- An earnings section which will describe in specific detail how the gross pay was calculated. There will be columns that will have the terms rate of pay, hours worked, amount earned this period and a year to date column showing your gross income for the current calendar year, January 1 through December 31.

There are two terms that you need to understand. The first one is 'gross' pay. *Gross pay* is the amount an employee has earned before income tax and other deductions are subtracted from his/her pay. Included in your gross pay may also be items such as commissions and bonuses. This is money you have earned BEFORE any deductions have been subtracted – not the actual amount of your paycheck. The second one is 'net' pay. *Net pay* is the amount of money that an employee actually receives after all the

1 http://www.irs.gov/app/understandingTaxes/jsp/tools_glossary.jsp

deductions have been subtracted. This is the amount that will be reflected on the paycheck.

It is important for you to review the information on your earnings statement very closely every time to insure that it is accurate and it correctly reflects the exact amount of time that you have worked. If you are an hourly employee, you should keep a separate time card or work log of your hours to compare this information to your earnings statement for accuracy. If you are considered a salaried employee, meaning that you are being paid a flat rate or 'salary' to perform your job, no matter how many hours you work, the gross pay will be calculated and normally remain the same from pay period to pay period. This type of pay is more common as you enter professions beyond high school and college. It is still advised that you check this information carefully each pay period to insure its accuracy.

When it comes to your gross pay this information should be fairly detailed in nature. There are laws and policies that companies need to follow, plus companies want to disclose detailed information so that you have a record to maintain in your files should you need it for any reason.

Deductions

Next, you should have a section that is normally titled 'deductions.' *Deductions* are the specific items that will be listed as 'subtractions' from your gross pay. According to the Merriam-Webster Online dictionary a deduction is "an act of taking away or something that is or may be subtracted from taxable income." [2]

There are several types of deductions, or *taxes*, that you will need to understand that may appear on your pay stub. Some deductions are mandatory such as:

Federal Income Tax - *Federal income tax* is the amount of money that is withheld or levied from your gross pay by the federal government. The Internal Revenue Service defines it as the following: The federal government levies a tax on personal income. Federal income tax provides for national

2 http://www.merriam-webster.com/dictionary/deduction

programs such as defense, foreign affairs, law enforcement, and interest on the national debt.[3]

Social Security Tax (FICA) - *Social security tax* is the amount of money that is withheld or levied from your gross pay and given to the Social Security Administration, which provides retirement benefits. The following is the official definition provided by the Internal Revenue Service: "It provides benefits for retired workers and their dependents as well as for the disabled and their dependents. Also known as the Federal Insurance Contributions Act (FICA) tax." [4]

Medicare Tax - *Medicare tax* is the amount of money that is withheld or levied from your gross pay and given to the Social Security Administration to be used for medical care provided to qualifying people over 65 years of age.[5] The Internal Revenue Service defines it as: "Money used to provide medical benefits for certain individuals when they reach age 65. Workers, retired workers, and the spouses of workers are eligible to receive Medicare benefits upon reaching age 65."[6]

State Income Tax - *State income tax* is the amount of money that is withheld or levied from your gross pay by the state in which you reside. (Some states do not have a state income tax, so you may not see this deduction on your paycheck or pay stub.)

Depending on the state in which you live, there may be other mandatory deductions that appear. These are questions that you can ask before you receive your first paycheck. At some point you will be given options to select other deductions such as medical care, dental care, life insurance, personal disability insurance and an assortment of retirement programs most commonly referred to as a 401(k) (or a *403(b)* if you work for a non-profit organization.)

---

3 http://www.irs.gov/app/understandingTaxes/jsp/tools_glossary.jsp
4 http://www.irs.gov/app/understandingTaxes/jsp/tools_glossary.jsp
5 http://www.answers.com/topic/medicare
6 http://www.irs.gov/app/understandingTaxes/jsp/tools_glossary.jsp

401(k) or Defined Contribution Plan

This is a good opportunity to discuss a very common and familiar term that you will encounter often as you begin working and move forward in your career. A *401(k)*, also know as a *defined contribution plan*, is a tax deferred retirement program established by your employer which allows you to set aside part of your salary or wages for retirement. There are limits on exactly how much you can contribute to a 401(k). Contact your human resources representative, a tax advisor or investment professional to understand the exact rules and regulations governing acceptable contribution limits.

Beyond your individual contribution for retirement, employers may also offer what is called a **full or partially matching program**. This means that as you elect to make contributions to your 401(k) account, your employer will 'match' or contribute a matching percentage to your account. This is 'free' money, as a benefit of working for them to encourage you to contribute to your retirement account. What a deal!

Important: When you are working for a company that offers a 401(k) ALWAYS SIGN UP! Consider participation to be mandatory, it is part of your job. A growing number of employers today are beginning to automatically enroll employees when they start working.

Company Matching Program

Here's why you want to participate. Let's look at an example of exactly what this means and how beneficial it can be for you. You have a job and you are making $36,000 per year. You choose to participate in your *company matching program*. As part of the company's 401(k) program they will match up to 6% of your salary.

You decide to contribute 6% of your salary (enough to take advantage of full matching), that's $2,160 or $180 per month. Your employer will match 6% and contribute for you another $2,160. That's a 100% rate of return on your money! To get a clearer understanding of what that additional matching amount means to you, assume that the money would stay invested for 40 years, earning an average of 8% a year. That additional $2,160 would earn a total of $50,271.51 in interest.[7] Think about it, where else can you find an investment vehicle that is going to provide you with 100% rate of return, outside of a 401k program? When you do please contact me so I can get in on it. As you can see, this is free money being given to you, take advantage of it. DO NOT WASTE THIS OPPORTUNITY BY NOT TAKING FULL ADVANTAGE OF IT! As you move ahead in your career(s), this will become clearer and will play an even greater role as you plan for your financial future.

Important: A company matching program is provided as a benefit by an employer. It is not a required benefit and may be discontinued, at the discretion of the company.

Two Golden Rules about Your 401(k)

Even though we are talking about working early in your life, it may seem premature that we would talk about having multiple jobs over your lifetime. However, in today's dynamic work environment it is likely you will have multiple jobs throughout your working life. As a result of this you will most likely be participating in more than one 401(k) retirement program. This has the potential of becoming financially damaging if not handled properly.

The **first golden rule regarding your 401(k)** account is that when you leave your employer and you are required to move your 401(k) account **YOU NEVER CASH OUT THE ACCOUNT!** This is a mistake far too common for people today. In a study conducted by the Employee Benefit Research Institute, 30 percent reported spending some or all of the money or using it to pay off debt and 26 percent put it into personal savings or investments, thereby sacrificing some of their savings in early withdrawal penalties.[8] The government gives you great tax breaks to encourage retirement savings, but if you use it for other purposes, you will pay harsh penalties and greatly reduce your overall retirement savings.

Instead of cashing out your account you have two options. If your

---

7 http://www.banksite.com/calc/savings.cgi?amt=2160.00&dep=0&cmp=Monthly&int=8.0&yrs=
8 EBRI Issue Brief No. 316 • April 2008 • www.ebri.org

employer allows terminating employees to leave the account at the current provider you can choose to do so. If they require departing employees to move the accounts you will want to transfer your 401(k) to an *Individual Retirement Account (IRA)* with a financial entity such as a bank, insurance company, full or discount brokerage company, etc. This process is very easy to complete; you will furnish transfer forms to your past 401(k) provider and they will handle the transfer to the new IRA account. It will be your responsibility to monitor the status of the transfer. Again, DO NOT CASH OUT THE ACCOUNT, including accepting a check directly to you. The money needs to be transferred directly to your new IRA account.

When you begin making contributions to your 401(k) account, you have made the conscious decision to focus on saving money for your retirement. This money should never be used for anything but that sole purpose. But because of rules and regulations pertaining to 401(k) accounts, most will offer an option for the accountholder to withdraw money as a loan to oneself.

This brings us to the **second golden rule regarding your 401(k)** account, **NEVER BORROW MONEY AGAINST YOUR 401(k)!** Your 401(k) account is not a personal savings account. It is for your retirement – period. People often borrow money from their 401(k) accounts when they find themselves in difficult financial situations without sufficient backup resources available. This behavior has the potential for you to incur fees, penalties and taxes and you will lose the growth of compounding interest. In essence it will make a bad situation worse.

In a recent survey conducted by Transamerica Center for Retirement Studies, there was an increase in the number of employees tapping into their accounts by taking out loans. The study showed that in 2007, 18% had taken out a loan, an increase from the 11% in 2006. Of those taking out loans, 49% indicated they used the money to pay off existing debt. This was a significant increase over 2006 which was still high at 27%.[9] Just think, these people are borrowing money to pay off money they have

---

9 Transamerica Center For Retirement Studies, 9th Annual Transamerica Retirement Survey – Workforce, www.transamericacenter.org, February 28, 2008.

already borrowed. When you think about this, do you really think this is a good financial strategy – taking money that you are planning on using for retirement and using it to pay off debt?

Catherine Collinson, a market and trends expert for the Transamerica Center for Retirement Studies says, "While a loan from your 401(k) plan seems like an obvious choice when you're in need of money, many are unaware that this short-term solution can often create more problems." She states further, "Once you terminate employment, most retirement plans require that you repay the loan in full or it will be considered a taxable distribution in which regular income tax applies and, if you are under age 59 ½, an additional 10 percent penalty applies."[10] As you can see the financial implications that can occur from borrowing money from your 401(k) can have devastating consequences. Stay with your strategy and set money aside for retirement and leave it alone - it's that simple.

The two golden rules of your 401(k) may not be relevant to where you are in your life at this moment, but they are very good rules by which to live. Remember and practice them when they do become applicable at certain stages in your life.

Pre-Tax Dollars

Let's briefly discuss a financial concept called ***pre-tax dollars***. Certain deductions will be subtracted that will reduce the amount of taxes to which you will be subjected in a manner called – pre-tax dollars. These **deductions will be subtracted from your gross pay before the appropriate tax,** according to federal and state tax guidelines, is calculated and deducted. This is a benefit to you because as your gross pay is decreased, the tax that is withheld will be less, meaning that you will get more money in your pocket instead of giving it to the federal and state governments. It is always in your best interest to take advantage of applying certain deductions on a pre-tax basis. This information will be available directly from your employer.

10 Transamerica Center For Retirement Studies, 9th Annual Transamerica Retirement Survey – Executive Summary, www.transamericacenter.org, February 28, 2008.

Paycheck

Typically when you begin employment you will have an actual check attached to the earnings statement. The money you have earned has been properly calculated into your net pay, which is the dollar amount that is indicated on your check. The dollar amount on the actual paycheck should match the dollar amount on the line called 'net pay.' This is the check that you will either deposit into your bank account or cash.

Note: It can be very difficult to go to just any bank and cash your check. The reason that it is so hard is that if you do not have an account with a bank they do not have 'recourse,' which is the ability to recover the money if, for some reason, the check is not good (or 'bounces.') This happens when the bank that you cashed the check with does not receive the money from the other bank that the check is drawn upon. You should be able to cash the check at the bank that the check is issued against or at your own bank once you set up an account.

Important: You will notice that I mentioned cashing your paycheck at a bank or depositing it at a bank. When you are just starting out, understanding the function of a bank provides a good foundation on which to build. **Under no circumstances do I condone or encourage you to EVER use a check cashing site (also know as payday lenders or cash advance centers) to cash your check. You have worked way too hard for your money to pay some business a fee so you can have your money quicker. DO NOT GET IN THIS HABIT.**

Direct Deposit

Another way to receive your money is by *direct deposit*. Your **net pay will be directly deposited electronically into your bank account**, either a checking or savings account. If you can, I strongly encourage you to utilize direct deposit because it will make things much easier for you, saving you an incredible amount of time by not having to stand in line at a bank or stop by a bank and use the ATM machine.

In order to receive your paycheck with direct deposit it is a very simple procedure. You will obtain a direct deposit form from your employer. Along with the form you will furnish a voided check or a savings deposit slip from your account that will have the *ABA routing number* (the number in the left hand corner of the check or savings deposit slip) and your account number. The employer will then set up your paycheck to be directly deposited into your account. Unless you already have an existing bank account and your employer is really on the ball, it is rare that your first paycheck will be available for direct deposit. Normally, your employer will inform you of the grace period or give you an estimate of when you will be able to receive your pay by direct deposit. This procedure has become so common that sometimes you will not even be given the option of a paper check. In those cases, you can rest assured that your employer will guarantee that you will receive your pay.

Important: When you receive your very first paycheck it is critical for you to review it and ensure its accuracy. Once you have verified that your paycheck or earnings statement is correct, you should maintain a separate file for them until the end of the year when you will receive a year end statement called a *W-2 Form - Wage and Tax Statement* (which we will discuss later when we talk about filing a tax return). At that point you can verify that all the information is correct. It is a good habit to keep them for your records for seven years.

If there is something listed on your earnings statement with which you are not familiar, ask immediately for an explanation – do not wait. Remember it is your paycheck and it is your responsibility to understand it - not your employers to hold your hand and explain it to you.

WOW! That was a lot of information and by far the most in-depth discussion that we have had thus far. You did a great job getting through it. It is important for you to gain a clear understanding of what your earnings statement is and what it means. It is your responsibility to ALWAYS manage and maintain your pay. It is one of the most important parts of not just your work life but your overall life. Remember, to be successful in planning your financial future, this is a critical component. Take a break you deserve it, or stay with me and we will move on.

Chapter 4

WHAT DO YOU MEAN, PAY YOURSELF FIRST?

As you make your way down the path to your financial future, you must develop personal money management skills. It is very important for you to grasp the concept that this is totally up to YOU.

Finally, I have money of my own. Now I can do what I want with my money without always having to ask someone else for it, I can spend it! Well, I know the first thing I am doing. I am taking it and I am going out to spend it all. Every day I keep seeing those really nice clothes in the window of Abercrombie and Fitch and those jeans at Lucky Brand. While I am walking I will stop in at the Apple store to check out the new iPods and upgrade mine or maybe just spring for the new iPhone – what the heck. I am living large today. Then I am going home with all of my new purchases, still riding my spending frenzy and getting myself some new music downloads from iTunes. I am so glad to have my own money.

This may all sound grand, it could even sound a little extravagant, and it might even sound a little far-fetched but in all reality – it isn't.

This is fairly normal behavior today for young adults when they finally have their own money. That is why we are going to discuss the concept of paying yourself first, before you get yourself into this frenzy.

You might be wondering, *"What do you mean, pay yourself first? Why do I have to pay myself first? Am I not going to get paid first when I get my check from my job? And if I get money from my parents or grandparents for a birthday or a holiday or some special occasion, I've already been paid; I am holding the money in my hand. So why do I have to pay myself first?"*

Paying yourself first is the act of putting aside money for specific purposes before anything else. This is a VERY important concept to understand because the rewards will be life altering, yet is very simple to do. The hard part is to consistently repeat the behavior over and over and over. There are many distractions, interruptions and temptations that can detour you off the path. That is why it is an extremely important habit to form early on.

'Pay yourself first' means that you are going to consciously set money aside. It will not matter if it is money from a job, a gift, a tax return or money that you inherit. By paying yourself first, you are responsible for taking care of yourself, watching out for YOU. Because, when it is all said and done – day in and day out – there is only one person that is really going to take care of you, and that is YOU! That is why you must develop the important habit of taking control of your life and specifically, your money. The following is the simple **Pay Yourself First Budget Worksheet** that outlines the basic formula to be used.

Pay Yourself First - Budget Worksheet

Money from working (Net Pay)
deposited to checking/savings $ ____
   10% Retirement Savings   - $ ____
Remaining money   = $ ____
   10% Savings Account   - $ ____
Remaining money   = $ ____
   10 % Charity of choice   - $ ____
Remaining money
in checking/savings account   = $ ____

Example

Money from working (Net Pay)
deposited to checking/savings $500.00
   10% Retirement Savings   - $ 50.00
Remaining money   = $450.00
   10% Savings Account   - $ 50.00
Remaining money   = $400.00
   10 % Charity of choice   - $ 50.00
Remaining money
in checking/savings account   = **$350.00**

Depositing Money

The first thing you will do is **deposit the money** you have received, from whatever source, into your checking or savings account. After that you will begin the pay yourself first process by allocating or setting money aside into the three predetermined accounts, retirement savings, a regular savings account, and a charity account with the remaining money in your account. Let's look at each account in detail.

Retirement Savings

As you will notice on the budget worksheets provided, the FIRST financial decision that you should make BEFORE ANYTHING is to take **10% of your net money and place it in your retirement savings**. This may involve accumulating the necessary funds needed to meet the minimum to open a mutual fund or Roth IRA account. (This will depend on the mutual fund company's account opening policies.) I know what you're thinking; I can hear you loud and clear – RETIREMENT? Why do I have to be thinking about that now? Remember you are developing personal money management skills, saving for retirement has to be one of those goals – no matter what age you are. You are going to get old and there is nothing you can do to stop it. You may not even remotely be thinking about it right now, but it will happen, it happens to ALL of us. The word retirement doesn't just mean that you're old; it's the time in your life that you are rewarded for all of your hard work, when you can stop working and enjoy life without the demands of having a career, raising a family and so on. I know it can be very hard for you to imagine right now. But I share with you a very heartfelt thought from an elderly person, named Gladys, who once said to me, "the hardest part of getting old is remembering what you did when you were young." You don't want to remember when you are old how you should have been better about saving money for retirement and discover it is too late.

Savings Account

The SECOND financial decision that you should make is to take another **10% of your net money and place it in a *savings account***. You do this to establish an account for those expenses that are planned. This money can be used for those purchases we talked about, those 'wants' that always come up in your life. Examples may include that new iPod, saving for a car, begin saving to cover your college living expenses or saving for a new cell phone with an awesome key pad that will make texting so much easier. If you are working hard to save for something you really want you may decide to save more than 10% to achieve your goal sooner.

Holiday Spending Example

Another savings example is budgeting for the holiday season. Your purchases can add up very quickly and soak up your cash. You might resort to what the majority of people do and charge it. To avoid this, you can set up a separate account into which you will set aside a specific amount of money each month or when you receive money, with the intention of purchasing gifts for your friends or family members. You will then set up a spending plan for each person, based on the amount you save and pay cash for the items, avoiding a potentially problematic financial situation. Credit cards should not be used for these items because it will create debt for you. You will have to repay that debt, taking money out of your future monthly budget. Here is an example of what I mean:

Credit Card Example – Holiday Spending

$500 @ 18%, minimum payment $20.00[1]
(Note: The example assumes that the minimum payment is being made.)

Year 1
Spend $500
11 months later $ 351.71 Balance remaining

Year 2
New Holiday Spending $ 500.00
New Principle Balance $ 851.71

Balance 11 months later $ 706.69 Balance remaining

Year 3
New Holiday Spending $ 500.00
New Principle Balance $1,206.69

Balance 11 months later $1,065.52 Balance remaining

Looking at this example, at the end of season #1 you would have a $500 balance. The interest rate is 18%. If you make the minimum payment of $20, each month, after 11 months you will still owe $351.71. When the

---

[1] Source: http://www.bankrate.com

next holiday season rolls around you will still owe money on the gifts that you purchased the year before. If you continue to do this until that balance is paid off it would take 85 months and you will pay $369.79 in interest. The total cost for the $500 worth of gifts would be $869.79.

Now look at what happens if you don't pay off the balance. You spend another $500 the following year and now the balance is $851.71. If you continue to make the minimum payment for the next 11 months you will owe a balance of $706.69. I am not going to go on and on, but you get the idea. If this behavior is repeated over and over you can see how the balance continues to grow until you eventually max out your card and you are no longer able to borrow any money. Planning ahead with a savings account eliminates this problem.

There are going to be numerous times in your life when you are going to want to satisfy the desire to have something special or to treat yourself with a reward of some kind. By taking the time to plan and set money aside you will both reward yourself and at the same time feel good about not having to burden your finances by borrowing money and acquiring debt. There are also going to be those 'unexpected' expenses or emergencies that are going to pop up from time to time. Being prepared and planning ahead will help alleviate the discomfort that will already be associated with the unfortunate circumstance that has taken place. Having financial peace of mind is a very comforting feeling when you find yourself in that situation.

Charity

The THIRD and final financial decision that you should make is the act of giving back. **Another 10% of your net money should be set aside for your favorite charity** for a *donation* (or gift) to support a specific cause or institution. This is anything to which you want to personally contribute in order to make a difference. This is called tithing, or if you want to get really fancy it can also be called philanthropy or donating to your favorite philanthropic choice. Try using that one around your friends to impress them. Yeah right, if you want them running away from you.

If you do some research, exploring your interests, you will find an organization that will match your needs and be thrilled to have your donation. There are literally thousands of organizations out there willing to accept your donation to help them achieve their mission. To give you an idea of the types of charities that are available **Charity Navigator** (America's largest independent charity evaluator) provides free financial evaluations of America's charities. Here is a list of popular charities:

CARE	www.care.org
PATH	www.path.org
Conservation International	www.conservation.org
City of Hope (and affiliates)	www.cityofhope.org
American Red Cross	www.americanredcross.org
Mayo Clinic	www.mayoclinic.org
Save the Children	www.savethechildren.org
International Rescue Committee	www.theirc.org
Remote Area Medical	www.ramusa.org

In addition to these charities, there are websites available that can assist in the identification of charities and their causes and missions, as well as link you to the organizations. They are:

Case Foundation	www.casefoundation.org
Guide Star	www.guidestar.org
Give	www.give.org
Charity Watch	www.charitywatch.org

Beyond contributing to the cause of your choice financially, charities would probably also welcome you to volunteer your time to assist them in their endeavors. **Volunteering is a wonderful way to feel good about yourself and give back to your community**. You never know when you may find yourself in a position where you will need a helping hand and you will be thankful to those who are there to help you in a time of need just like you did.

To show how the act of giving can have personal positive effects, according to a study by Vanderbilt University and the University of Michigan of 3,617 women and men found that those who reported participating in some sort of volunteer work were happier, less likely to be depressed and had better physical health than those who didn't.[1]

Importance of Giving Back

One of the most admirable human traits we have is the act of giving back. Setting aside 10% to help someone out or to offer assistance to an organization and its mission provides a very valuable and worthwhile experience. It will be far more than the actual physical act of giving the money; it will be the unbelievable feeling in your heart of giving back. Take the time to actually place your little mark on the world – that is what giving is all about. (If you want to really see the effect of giving back and how important and rewarding it can be on a very large scale, type the name Bill Gates, founder of Microsoft, into any search engine on the internet and read about the billions of dollars his foundation, The Gates Foundation, has donated to various causes across the entire world.)

This is a tough topic for a lot of people, because this is one aspect of the **budgeting** process that can be easily eliminated and the funds can very quickly be sucked into another area of your personal finances. But it is more than about just giving money; it is about being who we are, being human. We all need to remember that we are on this earth to protect and care for each other. That said, some people just do not have the means to do so, some people choose to ignore it and don't do anything, and then there are those individuals, like you I hope, that strive to make a difference. Generosity is yet another way of paying yourself first.

Paying yourself first is actually pretty complex. It is more than just a phrase or sentence; it's about developing a habit that involves action on your part. **It involves taking the initiative and responsibility to look beyond the present and toward the future by setting money aside**, be

---

1 Moser, Rachel. "Last Word." Woman's Day (ISSN 0043-7336), November 13, 2007, volume #71, issue #1. Hachette Filipacchi Media U.S. Inc., New York, New York

it from a job, a gift or a tax refund.

As you can see, '**paying yourself first**' is a valuable habit to form. Practice it wholeheartedly and you will see many good things come out of it. I hope you feel as great about it as I do. Once again, great job. Let's move on.

Chapter 5

I WANT TO SPEND, SPEND, SPEND

I have to say that this is probably my favorite topic to discuss throughout this entire program. I am in the minority, because this is by far the least popular subject with most people. Why? Because this is about limiting your temptation to spend money on a frequent basis. 'Spend, spend, spend' is what the majority of people love to do with their money. While I don't have anything against people who want to spend their money, I do have a problem with people who choose to spend their money without thought or planning. **Money must be spent in a systematic way, organized and categorized** or it will vanish into thin air, like a magic trick.

You are going to learn one of the most successful financial tools that will enable you to spend, spend, spend, but in a manner that you can manage and live with – one that will enable you to live within your means. It will provide happiness and satisfaction, along with sound personal money management skills, all while assisting you in achieving your financial goals. This important financial tool is called *budgeting*.

Budgeting

Budgeting is a long proven way for you to establish a road map; as if you were going on a vacation in your car and you wanted to know **how to get from point A to point B**. A budget will do the same thing, it will provide you with a starting point (money you have earned or been given) and then through a series of stops (financial obligations or bills) you will eventually end up at your destination (discretionary income or pure spending money). When we address this section, we are addressing the entire concept of budgeting, making financial decisions with the emphasis of moving you in a direction toward your financial goals. This may be centered on saving for specific purchases like a down payment for a car, paying down debt, new electronic devices, new clothes or just putting money in your savings account for the future with no specific purpose in mind. Remember that **budgeting is an ongoing, evolving activity** because as conditions change in your life, so too will your need to direct your money for different uses. If you treat any and all monies that you obtain with a clear and defined thought process you will make financial decisions that are always in YOUR best interest. You must **build a habit of managing your money**; it is a critical life skill you will develop.

When establishing your habit, you should sit down somewhere private and quiet – where you can really concentrate on the importance of this function. This is also a great opportunity for you to sit down with your parents and demonstrate to them that you are taking the initiative and responsibility to develop money management skills and your financial future. There is nothing that parents love to see more than their children taking responsibility for themselves in some form or fashion.

Pay Yourself First

The place to start when establishing your budget is with the money you have. This may be money that you have earned while working at a job or money that has been given to you for some reason. The money that you enter on this line will be the 'net' or the actual dollar amount that you receive. As we discussed in pay yourself first, the first financial decision is setting aside a minimum of **10% of your net money to be invested in a retirement account**. Next you should set aside another **10% of your net money in a savings account** for expenses that are either planned or unplanned. Finally you should set aside another **10% of your net money to be used as a donation to your favorite charity**. The money remaining is the money you will now begin budgeting to live on.

Fixed Expenses

Now looking at the middle of the budget worksheet, input your *fixed expenses*, the specific items that you must pay on a repeated basis, monthly, quarterly (every three months) or yearly. Here are some lists of basic expenses for which you may be responsible.

List #1 is for high school students living at home who have a part-time job. Here is a list of possible expenses:

- Credit card balance
- Charge card balance (retail stores)
- Cell phone
- Gasoline
- Auto insurance

List #2 is for young adults living at home who are working and/or attending college. Here is a list of possible expenses:

- Tuition
- School supplies/books
- Health care
- Student loans
- Credit card balance
- Charge card balance (retail stores)
- Car payment
- Auto insurance
- Gasoline
- Cell phone

List #3 is for young adults living on their own, either working and/
or attending college. Here is a list of possible expenses:

- Rent
- Tuition
- School supplies/books
- Health care
- Utilities (gas, water, electricity, cable TV, internet)
- Student loans
- Credit card balance
- Charge card balance (retail stores)
- Car payment
- Auto insurance
- Gasoline
- Cell phone
- Groceries
- Club membership/dues

The above lists provide you with a general idea of the types of
expenses for which you need to prepare. Some of them, I know, may be
brand new to you and frankly appear foreign, and you might have others
that are not listed, but use this as a guide to establish your budget and
include your own personal expenses.

Variable Expenses

Now we can look at the bottom of the budget worksheet. There are
variable (optional) expenses. These expenditures are not mandatory but
may be very important to you:

- Restaurants/eating out
- Entertainment (movies, concerts, sporting events, etc.)
- Music (CD's, downloads, etc.)
- Electronics, gaming software
- Clothing
- Travel expenses

There are multiple possibilities for building and maintaining your budget, and aspects of it will change from time to time. Concentrate on establishing limits for yourself when it comes to spending money. When you establish your budget and create appropriate categories for your money, you will be accurately managing your money in a smart and strategic manner.

In The Black

It is not a necessity to plan your budget to come down to a zero balance. When you effectively manage your money, there will be times when you will have funds remaining in your budget and the ending balance will be positive or '**in the black**.' A great habit to get into is to transfer the remaining balance to your savings account and then start the monthly budgeting process all over again. This will enable you to grow your savings account even faster for those 'wants' that you have: saving for that car, upgrading to a new iPod, socking away money to cover those upcoming college expenses or reaching that magic number, that minimum balance required to open up a mutual fund account and begin building your wealth. This takes some work and you will have to pay close attention, but if you can master it and use it on a consistent basis, you will save money at an even faster pace. You will start to become aware of your spending and be able to plan effectively. By doing so, you will be able to save more money and achieve your short term and long term goals more quickly.

In The Red

There is also the chance that your ending budget number will be negative or '**in the red**.' The bottom line is that your expenses are exceeding your income. When this happens you will have to look at the areas of your life where sacrifices can and need to be made. This is that part of budgeting people absolutely despise. This is when bad habits begin and the use of a credit card or multiple credit cards are substituted for money in order to continue the normal spending pattern. By forming this habit you are now establishing debt, which needs to be repaid, which in turn takes money out of your budget. Debt does not solve your problem and it launches you into a vicious cycle which can potentially lead you into financial disaster.

Cost of Living

Sometimes an economic event takes place which is beyond your control and it can have a significant impact on your budget. For instance, as I follow the news today, the price of oil is skyrocketing by record setting proportions. One may think, "So what, what's the big deal?" The reason is that it has HUGE ramifications on your budget. Let me explain how. Let's say you have a Honda Civic. The fuel capacity of the Civic is 12.3 gallons. You rely on your car as your primary means of transportation. You budget $49.20 (gas at $4.00 per gallon) to fill your tank and you fill it five times a month or $246.00 per month. If oil prices continue to increase it could now cost you about $55.35 week (gas at $4.50 per gallon) to fill your tank, the monthly cost increases to $276.75 a month. That is an increase of about 12% or $30.75. You might say to yourself, "its only $30.75." But remember that it doesn't stop there, it affects many other expenditures. Oil is used in making an abundance of products such as plastic, like the bottles for water or soda. It also makes other fuels including diesel fuel which is used to power vehicles that transport the majority of goods we consume. What does that mean? If the price of fuel increases, so does the cost of transportation that companies have to pay to transport those goods. The increased cost in fuel will then get passed on to the consumer by increased prices, resulting once again, in more money coming out of your pocket. If prices go up a couple dollars here and there that's a few more dollars you have to account for and that ultimately comes out of your overall budget. It starts to add up over time. As these uncontrollable, fluctuating expenses continue to increase, they begin to affect your budget.

A recent Los Angeles Times article entitled, "Bring the High Cost of Living Down to Earth" [1] examined common consumer products and

1 Ernest, Leslie. "Bring the High Cost of Living Down to Earth." Los Angeles Times, 9 March 2008, Sunday Business Section, Page 1.

services and their increasing costs. Here are the comparisons used on specific items:

- Self serve gasoline prices increased 26.9% from January 2007 to January 2008.
- Automobile maintenance costs increased 25.8% from 2006 to 2007.
- Bank fees increased 24.6% from the fall of 2006 to fall 2007.
- Grocery prices increased 7.1% from January 2007 to January 2008.

It may appear that these increases are slight, but each little increase adds up and takes money out of your pocket. Yet there is one thing that generally remains constant – your income. Unless you can work more hours or you are working on a commission, your salary or your hourly wages tend to remain fixed. When these **expenses** occur and your cash flow is fixed, you will have to make adjustments to other areas of your budget, meaning that you might have to **make sacrifices**. This could even mean getting a second job. When people don't make sacrifices, they often resort to pulling out those little plastic cards (credit cards) and begin to accumulate debt to maintain the same lifestyle, a potential for disaster. That is why it is so important to use a budget and to also review it on a regular basis so that you will not be caught off guard when uncontrollable expenses creep up on you.

Spend some time on this habit, keep working on it and improving upon it, and you will reap huge rewards. Let's continue.

Budget Worksheet
High school students living at home who have a part-time job

Money from working (net pay)
deposited to checking/savings $ _____

10% Retirement savings   - _____

Remaining money   = _____

10% Savings account   - _____

Remaining money   = _____

10 % to Charity   - _____

Remaining money deposited
to your checking account   = _____

Expenses:

Debt (credit card)   - _____

     = _____

Debt (charge card)   - _____

     = _____

Cell phone   - _____

     = _____

Gasoline   - _____

     = _____

Auto insurance   - _____

     = _____

Restaurants/eating out   - _____

     = _____

Entertainment   - _____

     = _____

Electronics (gaming/music)   - _____

     = _____

Clothing   - _____

     = _____

Discretionary funds/spending money $ _____

Budget Worksheet

Young adults living at home, working and/or attending college

Money from working (net pay)
deposited to checking/savings $ _____

10% Retirement savings   - _____

Remaining money   = _____

10% Savings account   - _____

Remaining money   = _____

10 % to Charity   - _____

Remaining money deposited
to your checking account   = _____

Expenses:

Tuition   - _____
   = _____

School supplies/books   - _____
   = _____

Health care   - _____
   = _____

Debt (student loan(s))   - _____
   = _____

Debt (credit card)   - _____
   = _____

Debt (charge card)   - _____
   = _____

Car payment (per month)   - _____
   = _____

Auto insurance   - _____
   = _____

Gasoline   - _____
   = _____

Budget - *Young adults living at home, cont.*

Cell phone   - _____

     = _____

Restaurants/eating out   - _____

     = _____

Entertainment   - _____

     = _____

Electronics (gaming/music)   - _____

     = _____

Clothing   - _____

     = _____

Groceries   - _____

     = _____

Travel (winter/spring break)   - _____

     = _____

Discretionary funds/spending money $ _____

Budget Worksheet

Young adults living on their own, working and/or attending college

Money from working (net pay)
deposited to checking/savings $ _____

10% Retirement savings   - _____

Remaining money   = _____

10% Savings account   - _____

Remaining money   = _____

10 % to Charity   - _____

Remaining money deposited
to your checking account   = _____

Expenses:

Rent   - _____
    = _____

Tuition   - _____
    = _____

School supplies/books   - _____
    = _____

Health care   - _____
    = _____

Utilities   - _____
    = _____

Debt (student loan(s))   - _____
    = _____

Debt (credit card)   - _____
    = _____

Debt (charge card)   - _____
    = _____

Car payment (per month)   - _____
    = _____

Budget -*Young adults living on their own, cont.*

Auto insurance   - _____

                                            = _____

Gasoline   - _____

                                            = _____

Cell phone   - _____

                                            = _____

Restaurants/eating out   - _____

                                            = _____

Entertainment   - _____

                                            = _____

Electronics (gaming/music)   - _____

                                            = _____

Clothing   - _____

                                            = _____

Groceries   - _____

                                            = _____

Travel (winter/spring break)   - _____

                                            = _____

Discretionary funds/spending money $ _____

Budget Worksheet
Gift money

Gift money	$	_____
10% Retirement savings	-	_____
Remaining money	=	_____
10% Savings acct.	-	_____
Remaining money	=	_____
10 % to Charity	-	_____
Remaining money		
In your checking account	=	_____

Note: Budget worksheets are online at www.michaeljwagner.net

Chapter 6

CALLING 911 WON'T HELP

Through this program, it is my intention to assist young adults in developing personal money management skills to plan for their financial future by budgeting well and avoiding financial pitfalls. Another way to provide for your financial well being is establishing an *emergency fund*. Because you are young it might be difficult to imagine what such an emergency might be, but I would not be doing you any favors by neglecting this very important and often overlooked issue.

Emergency Fund

An emergency fund is simply money that is set aside to be used in case of an emergency. When we talk about an emergency, we don't mean that you are trying to get ready to go out for a night on the town and you don't have anything cool to wear. Or, for example, when my stepson called from the local guitar shop saying, "Oh, you wouldn't believe it, my favorite Les Paul guitar is on sale *only* this week. It's never going to be this cheap again." When asked, "How much is it and how do you plan to pay for it?," he replied, "It is only like $800 and I can put it on layaway." He said he could borrow the money from us (his parents) and pay us back (an interesting concept since he didn't have a job). People might argue that this is a real emergency, but it isn't – sorry. An **emergency** is an event or events that will significantly impact your life, your current financial status, as well as your financial future.

Types of Emergencies

The types of events that an emergency fund might be used for are things like being laid off from your job, your work hours being reduced, or quitting your job. You could develop a serious illness or become injured and disabled for a period of time or you might incur *unexpected expenses* from an auto accident. Let me share an example.

Someone hits your car and leaves the scene without leaving you any information. There is nothing worse than approaching your car and seeing broken glass or a huge dent and scratches on your car. There you stand, looking around in disbelief and there is not a sole in sight. Great! Now you have to either fix it by spending money out of your pocket or contact your insurance company, which means paying a deductible, the amount you are responsible to pay before the insurance company will pay its portion. Plus there is the time you will spend dealing with the situation which ultimately could affect your work hours, in addition to leaving you without your car while the repairs are being made, meaning you may have to rent a car. You get the picture.

Why Do I Need One?

Often your emergency is the result of something that you had nothing to do with, like parking your car in the wrong place at the wrong time, or other incidents like fires, earthquakes or floods. You are probably thinking that you aren't going to start a fire in your own apartment, but remember, if you are living in an apartment building, there are other people that could be responsible, or should I say irresponsible, and if they start a fire you could be at risk of losing your possessions or having some kind of damage. Even with insurance coverage, you will still have out-of-pocket expenses to contend with.

Just the other day I was visiting with a young girl who worked at a local coffee shop. I was in the shop when she opened her paycheck, to her dismay; she was not happy with her check. When I asked her about it she told me that she had left another job to take this one so she could make more money. Unfortunately, because of some extenuating circumstances beyond her control (a reduction in customers and sales) the business began implementing measures including reducing both the store's operating hours and employee hours. This impacted her because she was now working less and earning less than she was at her previous job. An emergency fund would have helped her bridge the gap until she could resolve her situation.

Another emergency that is all too common is the unfortunate situation of becoming **unemployed**. This can happen to the best of us, not just being fired from your job, but also being laid off because of some unforeseen circumstance. This might be a business that is dependent upon the survival of another industry. For example, the mortgage issues that plagued most of the United States in 2007 resulted in a vast number of financial institutions laying off employees as a result of a slow down of the home mortgage industry and of people purchasing homes. As the slow down occurs, it has a domino effect and others that are dependent on the mortgage industry, such as realtors, brokers, title companies and appraisers, begin to suffer as well. Business drops off or slows down, as does their work, and they get laid off or their incomes are significantly reduced, thus impacting their personal financial situations. When this occurs, financial decisions must be made. The impact of being ill-prepared can have disastrous, life altering effects that can damage one's financial situation, and one's personal credit standing.

One of the major mistakes people make establishing an emergency fund is that they don't actually think about it or plan for it saying, "Oh, it won't happen to me." The other decision that people make is to utilize some type of credit borrowing as an emergency fund. The problem with this plan is that you may not have sufficient credit limits to take care of your needs. Also, if your emergency leaves you unable to work, you will be borrowing money that you will have to begin repaying right away, creating another financial problem. As you can see, it won't take much for the situation to get out of control.

That is why you must establish an emergency fund to assist you in the time(s) of need. Hopefully, you will not have to experience this situation on a repeated basis throughout your life, but if you do, preparation will help you deal with it without an unfortunate financial situation compounding your troubles.

Where Do I Start?

How do you go about establishing an emergency fund and how do you determine how much money you should save or set aside? The key to establishing an emergency fund is not any different than we have already discussed. It is just another part of the ever so important budgeting process. It is going to take discipline to be able to set aside, each and every month, an amount of money that will get you to your **emergency fund goal**. How should you go about setting up a fund? Use the K.I.S.S. principle. K.I.S.S. stands for Keep It Short & Simple. Set up a **savings account**, in which the money that you deposit is going to earn interest on a regular basis. One key point about an emergency fund is that the money needs to be 'liquid.' This means that you will want to be able to withdraw the money right away and not invest the money in an account that will take time to access. For example, a mutual fund may take days or weeks to cash out and can lose its value. Certificates of deposit (CDs) may have penalties for early withdrawal. However, the money that you are saving should earn interest, even though the purpose is to use it in case of an emergency. This is why a savings account is usually the best choice for an emergency fund.

How Much Do I Need?

The next part of establishing an emergency fund is determining how much money you should save. There are many schools of thought on what the proper amount of money is. A basic guideline is to **determine your total living expenses on a monthly basis**. This will be easy since you have already established a **monthly budget**, with the budget worksheets provided. Once that number is determined, the general rule of thumb is that you should use three to six months of personal living expenses as an emergency fund goal. These are the expenses in the middle of your budget worksheet. Once you determine this amount you can make the necessary decisions and adjustments to get the fund started. Remember that once you have established the emergency fund and you have reached your goal, you can redirect the money you have been putting into this account to other areas of your budget.

Health Insurance

I realize that you are at the point in your life right now where you are young, full of life, enjoying everything to its fullest. It is hard to imagine that a serious medical condition could occur that would interrupt it. This could result from something simple, like being injured participating in a recreational sport, to something more serious, like a car accident. As a result of increasingly exorbitant medical costs today, suffering from even the slightest medical issue could have serious financial ramifications if you are not prepared. To prevent yourself from being placed in this position, understand how important it is to **ALWAYS maintain health insurance coverage.** If you are a teenager (under the age of 18) you are probably covered under your parent's health coverage. Once you graduate from high school and you either go to college or you enter the working world, this situation may change. You may continue to be covered by your parent's health insurance, you may have an insurance benefit with your job or you may need to be covered under your own policy. Most colleges will have health centers that will assist you if you have common ailments but for major illnesses you will be on your own. It is imperative that you understand how being properly covered is a necessity. Without proper insurance coverage and without the proper savings established, you create the potential to find yourself in a situation that could have severe financial consequences.

An **emergency fund is a vitally important** financial principle and as you get older, it will play an even more pivotal role in your life. This is an issue that far too many people overlook while developing a budget and living their lives, but ignoring it can single-handedly place you in a very difficult financial position, and might even put you in financial ruin for a very long time. Planning for possible misfortune is one of many skills that will benefit you in your life. Moving right along.

Chapter 7

HOW DID THEY FIND ME?

We have been talking about the importance of developing personal money management skills. The reason that personal money management is so important is that it affects all areas of your life and provides a path of opportunities for you to lead a life of fulfillment and happiness. I know, you are probably thinking right now, "Blah, blah, blah, I am young and I just want to have fun, live life, party and I will worry about all that other stuff later." Well, you are already being sucked into life's temptations: those things that play into your inner wants and desires, that make you want to spend money, be crazy and do whatever you want, forgetting about responsibilities. Experiencing that high can make us feel full of life and puts a smile on our face. However, it is quite like having a dream in which everything seems perfect, giving you a feeling of utter utopia, and then BAM, you get that jolt, that feeling as though you are falling. That is what *temptation* can result in, it looks great to the eye at first glance, but then you act upon it and when your rational mind finally kicks in you realize that the end result of acting upon your desire is not what you thought it would be. In the end it wasn't worth it and now you are stuck with the results of that decision.

The Hypnotic Trance

Well, believe it or not, that is what happens when credit card companies begin their relentless bombardment and never ending pursuit of you. They try to tap into that emotional state and break you down. It's as though you go into a **hypnotic trance** in which they wave the credit card mailing envelope in front of you from side to side, while at the same time chanting a subliminal message:

"Watch the envelope, watch the envelope; your eyes are getting heavy, watch the envelope. Now open the envelope, read the letter from the Vice President of Marketing." (with the fake embossed signature from a person that has no clue who you are and doesn't care.)

Somewhere within this letter it will say in bold, **"You have been pre-approved for a $2,000 credit line."** It will tell you that if you act now, you will receive special benefits or something **free.** (There is that word.) For example, zero percent interest on any purchases for the first six months. They should just say, "Go out and spend a bunch of money for the next six months and then when you are done you will owe us money for the next 220 months." [1] They continue to try to put you in this state chanting, "Your eyes are heavy" as you continue to read the letter and see all the fabulous features and benefits of having the credit card. Now all you have to do is take the credit card application and fill in the information. To be clear, they will be asking you for every bit of personal information to pull a credit report and see if you actually qualify to have a credit card. This information will include your name, address, social security number (which by the way is one of the most important pieces of personal information to keep secure), birth date, any income information

---

1 Based on borrowing $2000 at 18% and making the minimum payment until the balance is zero.

and then the kiss of death or 'the seal of approval' as I like to call it – your signature. By signing, you are providing the official go ahead to process your application. Your eyes are heavy, you are making movements you won't recollect the next day, which include sending the application back to the credit card company.

You may think that this story is far-fetched, but there are millions, yes, millions of people who do it all the time. And then guess what? The same day you walk to the mailbox and mail the application there is another one or even two more applications in your mail just like the one you just completed. **Credit cards are the epitome of temptation** to humans and credit card companies try to reach them at their weakest moments. Once you provide your personal information to anyone, that information is out there in the public. Companies sell that information to other companies, who then put you on their mailing list and bombard you with more direct mail, more temptation. When we registered my then, 14 year old stepson for a frequent flyer account with a major airline, he began to receive countless direct mailings from credit card companies stating that he was 'pre-approved.' Needless to say, they will not actually extend credit to a minor.

Retail Charge Cards

Often, retail stores will offer *charge cards* that will entice you with an on-the-spot incentive of a percentage off of your current purchase if you apply for the card and charge what you are purchasing. It is often required as part of the job as a sales associate to try to get you to fill out the application. Department stores, as well as banks and financial institutions, track the referrals of employees for sales incentives and awards. This is going to happen all the time at stores that you frequent; get in the habit of saying "No, thank you." There is no need for you to maintain a bunch of credit cards that really do nothing but provide you with the temptation to buy more. Plus, the more information you provide the more they will bombard you with direct mailing offers creating further temptation. It is an easy habit to get into; say, "No thank you, I am not interested."

Owning a Credit Card

You are probably asking yourself, "What's the big deal, so what, they want me to get a credit card, don't I need a credit card to be able to buy things and to build my credit rating?" Yes you do, but let's talk about what it means to have a credit card. A credit card is issued by a bank or business that allows the holder (you) to purchase goods and services on credit, meaning money is being lent to you by the bank or business that granted you the card. This enables you to buy something and repay them at a later date, in a lump sum or over a period time, with interest. The interest is the amount of money the bank or business charges you for lending you the money. (We will be discussing the repayment of this debt, in more detail, in a later section.)

Throughout this book I have made it clear that it is essential for you to develop the habit of reading everything that pertains to your financial situation. When you enter into a contract or agreement, such as obtaining a credit card account, it is *critical* that you read and understand exactly what the **terms and conditions** are for the account. When you are able to apply and are approved for a credit card, either on your own or with the help of your parents, do your research. If you are looking for some guidance and assistance in researching credit card companies and reviewing specific features to compare credit cards, try these websites:

www.creditcards.com
www.bankrate.com
www.credit-cards-info.com
www.creditcardguide.com

These sites offer a plethora of information pertaining to the credit card industry.

You will see many credit card companies offering incentives to apply for their card. They might offer a product if you sign up; they might offer '0%' interest for a certain amount of time (and when the time expires the rate may go to some astronomical figure.) This is a good opportunity to draw upon your relationship with your bank since they already have you as a customer and want to keep you. Banks do not like to lose customers! Banks have a harder time obtaining a new customer than retaining an existing customer. However, your bank may not always have the best deal, so do your research and only deal with reputable companies, ones that will have excellent customer service accessibility in case you have questions or problems.

Types of Credit Cards

The two major credit card companies that you will see associated with banks and credit card providers are **VISA** and **MasterCard**. They operate in conjunction with thousands of financial institutions that market their products worldwide. They are both internationally known and are widely accepted all over the world. To give you an idea of the size of these companies, the data provided by Creditcards.com[2] shows the market share of the top credit card companies:

Visa – 46 percent

MasterCard – 36 percent

American Express – 12 percent

Discover Card – 6 percent

(Source: Nilson Report, May 2008)

The third largest company, **American Express**, was founded in 1850. It is considered a global financial services company that offers credit card, financial and travel services. American Express also offers financial advice and retirement planning services.[3] They are similar to VISA[4] and MasterCard,[5] in that they are internationally known and also widely accepted. However, American Express[6] operates as its own financial services company, directly delivering its products and services where as VISA and MasterCard work in a partnership with banks and

2 http://www.creditcards.com/Parents-Play-Selection-Role.php
3 http://www.home.americanexpress.com
4 http:// www.usa.visa.com
5 http://www.mastercard.com
6 http://www.home.americanexpress.com

other financial services companies to offer their products and services. To give you an idea of just how big the credit card industry has become since the first issuance of the American Express card in 1958 and the first VISA card in 1977, (originally called the BankAmericard in 1959), in 2006 there were 984 million bank-issued VISA and MasterCard credit cards and debit cards in the United States.[7]

The fourth most popular credit card company is **Discover**,[8] the youngest of the four originating in 1985. Its business operation is similar to American Express in that they directly issue cards to consumers. Discover also offers a variety of products and services in addition to just credit and debit cards including home loans, savings products, insurance and student loans.

In 2006, the top ten credit card issuers controlled approximately 88% of the credit cards issued according to the Federal Deposit Insurance Corporation (FDIC).[9] Here is a list of the top ten credit card issuers:

Bank of America	JP Morgan Chase
Citigroup	American Express
Capital One	Discover Card
HSBC	Washington Mutual
Wells Fargo	US Bancorp

To continue to give you an idea how this little 2 inch by 3 inch plastic card has become overwhelmingly popular in the current consumer world, according to the **Federal Reserve** in November 2008 total U.S. consumer revolving debt, money owed by consumers on credit accounts, was almost $973 billion.[10] That was an increase of $98 billion from the $875 billion owed at the end of 2006. In comparison, in 1997 the amount owed was $554 billion, an increase of over $400 billion in just ten years.[11]

7 http://www.creditcards.com/Parents-Play-Selection-Role.php
8 http://www.discovercard.com
9 http://www.creditcards.com/Parents-Play-Selection-Role.php
10 http://www.federalreserve.gov
11 http://www.nacba.org/files/new_in_debate/Credit_Card_Debt_Bankruptcy.pdf

Rewards

As credit cards have gained in popularity and competition has become fierce, **program incentives** have been developed and are a popular way to provide you with 'rewards' or 'points' for using the credit card. You have the ability to accumulate incentives and use them for products or services they provide. For instance, American Express offers points associated with the use of their card. Once you accumulate a certain level of points they can be redeemed or exchanged with their partners for electronics, hotel stays, airline tickets and much more. Almost all the major airlines partner with financial institutions. When you sign up for their credit card they will offer an incentive providing points, which are equivalent to miles, with the airline. There are also cards which will give a certain percentage back to you in cash, which is applied to your account balance. When reviewing incentive programs, always understand the expiration policies. Incentive or reward programs often have expiration clauses written into the credit card agreements that if rewards, miles or points are not redeemed by a certain date they will expire. In other words, "Use 'em or lose 'em." There is no gain in accumulating points and not being able to take advantage of them. It is your responsibility to monitor and pay close attention to your accounts, if you want to take advantage of what you have rightfully earned. If you use a PDA or some type of computerized calendar, place the expiration date and a short explanation in the system to remind you.

If you are going to establish a credit card account you need to totally understand all the policies associated with the card and the nuances of the incentive program for which you have applied.

Self Control

You will be inundated with credit card offers on a more than frequent basis. You will have to develop a very strong *discipline* to resist the temptation that these companies will offer you ALL THE TIME. Credit card companies make money when you have and use your card. When you maintain a balance with accruing interest, it could potentially take you a very long time to repay and eliminate the debt. The only way they can make that happen is by getting a card in your hands; that is why it is so easy to obtain multiple cards. Multiple cards lead to multiple balances that lead to multiple payments. Mismanagement can and will lead you further away from the financial success and well being you both want and deserve. The world is filled with technology that has made it very easy for us to operate daily without the use of cash and writing a check has become almost obsolete. There are positive ways that credit cards assist us in our daily lives. I am not against the use of credit cards but I stress to you that it takes a strong personal commitment to be able to properly manage them. Great job, let's move on.

Chapter 8

YOU WILL NEED MORE THAN AN UMBRELLA: SAVING FOR RETIREMENT

I have a feeling that this section might not overly thrill you, how could it? Stop and take a moment and fast forward to when you are 60 years old. Yeah right. When I try to explain anything to my stepson and he doesn't want to hear about it or take the time to discuss something I deem as important (which is a lot of the time), he says, "I know, I got it." What do I expect? He is a 15 year old teenager – he knows everything. In my experience with young adults I find this parent-child interaction to be fairly common. This is his way of saying that he is not even remotely thinking about anything that is so far off, like his life at 60 years old. I really believe that he represents the general attitude of young adults in today's world.

The Value of Time

The world is moving forward, like it or not, and so is your own personal world. By this I mean you age, year by year. Soon your birthday celebrations will heat up the room with the amount of candles that will be on your birthday cake each year, (not to mention the size of the cake getting bigger to be able to fit all them on it). We have to plan for the future even when it seems so far away. It seems that there is plenty of *time* but before you know it that precious commodity has passed by and we have lost time that can NEVER be made up. This chapter is without a doubt, one of the most important because this is when you have to really look at taking control of a piece of your life that is hard to grasp and put your arms around it. You are being asked to look at something that is not going to happen for over forty years, FORTY YEARS. When I sit here and think about it, I have seen so much happen during that time period and I can't even imagine what you will see. But there is one thing that we can see together. You will be moving towards that time period called the *golden years*, that time when you will be considering retiring from the workforce and living out your life. I am not trying to get you to go through every conceivable scenario, but I am asking for you to accept that you are going to be aging and that you will need to be properly prepared, financially, for that time. You need to **utilize time to its fullest** so that you will have the opportunity to look back at your life that has passed by and smile. No matter if you like it or not, financial decisions that you can control and make today will have an unbelievable impact on this part of your life. If you want to remember one really important thing from this program it is that. To coin another phrase that you might have heard your parents use, **"don't put off until tomorrow what you can do today."**

A Rainy Day

Why did I say that you will need more than an umbrella at this point in your life? When you accept that you will eventually reach old age, even though it seems incredibly far off right now, it will help you tremendously. 'Saving for a *rainy day*' is about saving for when you are retired. When it comes, you need to have practiced the important habits and money skills so that you will not be standing out in the rain (reaching the age of 60 +) without having successfully planned for your financial future. Understand that by establishing the **proper financial planning habits**, your entire financial well being will drape over you like a sturdy umbrella.

Take Control

When it comes to talking about **retirement** and especially the aging process, remember that retirement is not just about being old and having to alter your life style because your age limits your ability to do things. Retirement can be achieved by many at an earlier age, sometimes in their 40's or 50's. But in order to take advantage of being able to enjoy a life like that, it is essential that you understand what it will take to accomplish this. I am not here to lecture you, but to encourage and mentor you to believe in yourself. You have the ability to take control of the life you want to have for yourself and your family. You can create a positive financial future by doing one thing – understanding the **importance of planning**. Having the ability to understand what the future will bring and what you are going to do with your money will become clearer as time goes on. As time goes by you will be able to see the rewards of your efforts, even during times that maybe tough or hard. It will pay off and the end result can be many years of happiness and fulfillment. In other words 'the long term gains will be far outweighed by the short term discomfort.' Having the perseverance to strive toward your established financial goals and forging ahead during those difficult times to that pot at the end of the rainbow will be worth it when it is all said and done. Sometimes, we lose focus of our specific long term goals when the desire to satisfy all of our immediate needs and wants gets in the way and it takes us off our path. When we finally decide to get back on it we realize that we have lost the most valuable ingredient to the financial future and that is time. It all keeps coming back to the issue of time.

Retirement Savings Calculator

Preparation is a critical element for financial success. It is the planning process that establishes the habits needed to build an effective savings program. One tool that can be used as a guide to assist you is a savings calculator. A *retirement savings calculator* program asks detailed information and then provides an answer based on your personal situation. Depending on the extent of the information asked the answer can range from very generic to specific. A savings calculator is proven to be an effective tool in the modification of changing savings behavior.

A recent survey conducted by the Employee Benefits Research Institute showed that 44% of those surveyed who calculated a goal changed their retirement planning and savings habits. As a result of changing their planning, 59% started saving and/or investing more money. Other changes included, changing their retirement mix (20%), reducing debt or spending (7%), enrolling in a retirement savings plan at work (5%), deciding to work longer (3%) and researching other ways to save for retirement (3%).[1]

This tool prepares individuals to begin looking beyond their immediate needs in life and take action that both involves and complements developing savings habits early. When using a savings calculator keep in mind it is only an estimate based on the information you provide. It provides necessary food for thought in preparing a savings plan. **Those who choose to use a savings calculator are far ahead of many others**. Of those surveyed, asked what method they used to determine their savings needs for retirement, an astounding 43% of respondents 'guessed.' Yes – guessed or as I like to say SWAG. (When I was in college a professor taught me what the acronym SWAG meant. Some Wild A** Guess.) Now ask yourself, when you are preparing for one of *the* most important phases of your life, is guessing really a proven method of effectiveness to make sure you are going to be prepared? I don't think so.

I know that you may be at a point in your life that retirement is not even in your thought pattern. However, as I have stated from the beginning, this is a resource for you to **develop effective money saving habits and sound personal money management skills** to use both now and in your future. To find a savings calculator, check on the internet by entering in a search engine, 'retirement savings calculator.' While a retirement savings calculator may not be something you will use right this second, you can

---

1 http://www.ebri.org/publications/ib/index.cfm?fa=ibDisp&content_id=3903

become familiar with its purpose so as you progress in your life you will become comfortable with how to use this valuable tool to your benefit.

Leave It Alone

Let's concentrate on **developing the habits** needed to successfully move you in the right direction. It is through the **budgeting process** that you build the habit of paying yourself first in establishing a retirement savings account. This is an account that you will deposit money into with the full understanding and intention to NEVER withdraw money from it for ANY purpose other than when you have reached the age of retirement. This account will be a separate account in which you will deposit money on a consistent basis, funds specifically earmarked, only to be used when you retire. This account will be something that you will monitor at a minimum on a quarterly basis. This will be a step in helping you develop a very important trait, one that will benefit you in many areas of your life, and that is – *patience*. There will be many times throughout your life that situations and events will tempt you to tap into this money, either withdraw it and spend it, or move it to another type of investment. **Patience** is one of the hardest things to achieve when you are trying to plan for your financial future. But remember you have one commodity on your side – time. **Time and patience will lead you to successful investing**. There will be a time in your life when you will want to consider moving the money you have saved, called reallocating, but for now, this is not something about which you need to be concerned. Your only concern should be to establish an account and develop the habit of saving money on a consistent basis.

You will need to have more than an umbrella to cover you with the protection you need from all the 'elements' of the aging process. To reinforce what has been discussed, I would empower you to talk to a person that is currently 50 or 60 years old and ask them if they have saved enough money for their retirement. Get their thoughts and ideas and relate to them what has been discussed. This could be a great real life lesson that could add insight. Thanks for hanging in there with me. Let's continue!

Chapter 9
_____

WHAT IS A MUTUAL FUND AND WHY DO I NEED IT?

W e have discussed a variety of reasons why it is important and the ways to establish a savings program. There are probably a lot of adults that could also utilize this information, especially when you think about the staggering number of people that file **bankruptcy**, have massive bills and credit card payments or those who are just living paycheck to paycheck. Let's change the trend and discuss ways to save money. It is possible to use various types of savings products to establish a financial portfolio. Regular savings accounts are good for short term needs, as well as an emergency fund for unexpected circumstances. However, when it comes to investing for your future retirement we will focus on utilizing mutual funds. *Mutual funds* are one of the simplest and most common ways to begin establishing an investment portfolio, while at the same time creating *diversification* or not placing all your eggs (money) in one basket.

We could seriously discuss the topic of mutual funds for a very long time. Go into the business section of a bookstore, you will see numerous shelves of books about a variety of investment topics and strategies, including mutual funds. The information provided here is just the basics to get started. We will cover what a mutual fund is, the key terminology, recognizing and choosing a proper fund, and developing enough knowledge to speak with an ***investment advisor***. It would be impossible (unless you want volumes of materials), and simply impractical to cover the multitude of investment options available to you. It will take time and experience to become a savvy investor, but learning some basic options is a great way to get started. Please note that as we discuss the following information there will be a variety of investment terms used. If you need further clarification of any terms please refer to the glossary.

We are going to concentrate on mutual funds because it is an excellent way to learn, understand and become an investor in the stock market. The stock market has been around for a very long time and, despite its ups and downs, has proven over the long term to produce financial growth. As you familiarize yourself with a mutual fund growth chart, one thing to always keep in mind is through all of the turmoil and world events (world wars, financial crises, 9/11) the stock market has been able to weather the storm and continue to provide an environment for people to earn more and build wealth.

Welcome to Wall Street

As a mutual fund owner you will be a stockholder. A mutual fund is an investment that brings together money from many people, just like yourself, to be invested in many companies. Each investor owns *shares* in the mutual fund and therefore becomes a shareholder of multiple companies. A mutual fund company hires a fund manager, ultimately your 'expert,' who will select and organize certain investments into a *portfolio*. This person is a professional with a vast amount of stock market expertise, other general business experience and formal education. The fund manager's responsibility is to act on your behalf by making the appropriate financial decisions that meet the overall goals, objectives and strategies that have been established for the fund.

The fund manager chooses a mix of ***stocks*** from companies that will be outlined in what is called the ***industry holdings*** for the fund. The companies are then grouped by the sector of business they compete in such as, information technology, pharmaceuticals, finance, telecommunications, energy, health care, consumer staples, etc. It is also possible to own a mutual fund that will have a group of fund managers called portfolio counselors. These are individual fund managers brought together that have varied experience and expertise who work on managing the fund together.

Owning mutual funds is consistent with your retirement objectives of looking long term, staying the course and staying invested. Catherine Collinson, the president of the Transamerica Center for Retirement Studies states, "The real secret of building a retirement nest egg is saving over the long term on a consistent basis."[1] Mutual funds typically demonstrate a buy and hold policy when it comes to owning investments consistent with a sound retirement savings strategy. They also offer a wide variety of funds that have different investment goals and objectives, which makes developing a portfolio with **diversification** easy. As a mutual fund owner you are embarking upon becoming an investor and can follow what financial experts have said is a key in building wealth, "Be invested, stay invested."

Evaluation

When you evaluate the type of mutual fund that will meet your investment goals and objectives, it is important to look at a variety of criteria in order to choose the appropriate one. The following is a concise list comprising the necessary elements in evaluating a mutual fund to start your portfolio:

- Establish your personal investment goal

- Determine your time horizon

---

1 http://www.articles.moneycentral.msn.com/RetirementandWills/InvestForRetirement/WorkersStepUpRaidsOn401ks.aspx

- Know your level of risk

- Select the type of investment category or fund classification

- Understand the fund's investment objective

- Analyze the past performance of the fund

- Consult the Morningstar rating system

- Decide on a load or no-load mutual fund

- Know the fees and minimum opening balance requirements

- Obtain and read the prospectus

This is a snapshot of what is really involved in the evaluation process of choosing a mutual fund. Let's take a look at each of these steps in more detail.

Investment Goal

When beginning any savings program it is important to first establish an investment goal. Your *investment goal* should include a specific purpose for the money that is being saved and may include a dollar amount. Your goals can be short term (a new laptop, iPod, down payment for a car, a vacation, deposit for an apartment, future college expenses, etc.) or long term (down payment for a house, college education.) Your investment goal of saving for retirement may not have a specific dollar amount to start. You will create the roadmap that will help you determine what type of investment will best suit your needs and objectives based upon both the time horizon and the level of risk you can tolerate. In this chapter we will be concentrating on saving for retirement using mutual funds while utilizing a long term time horizon.

Time Horizon

As a young adult, you have a long retirement *time horizon* (probably over 40 years.) This is the amount of time that you have available for the money to be invested in your account before you intend to begin using the money. Your account may incur market irregularities or a decrease in overall value as a result of a variety of economic business conditions that can occur, but should ultimately grow substantially over time. This money is going to be invested for over 40 years.

Risk

A primary factor in selecting a mutual fund is assessing how much risk you are willing to accept. *Risk* means how much market fluctuation you are willing to tolerate and how much money you are willing to potentially lose in your account. Of course, none of us wants to lose money, and when you are investing you want to be able to have peace of mind that the money is going to grow and increase in value over time. (Your fund manager will want the same thing. Fund performance is a large part of their compensation or pay they receive and it is partially based on how well the fund does. The better it does the more moolah they get. There is not a professional fund manager out there trying to lose your money on purpose.) There are three levels of risk under which mutual funds are classified, *aggressive/high*, *moderate/medium* and *conservative/low*: [2]

Aggressive/High - will accept above average market and price fluctuations to seek above average returns.
(Stock Funds)
Moderate/Medium - will accept average market and price fluctuations to pursue higher returns.
(Asset Allocation/Target Date Funds–a mix of all three risk levels)
Conservative/Low - will accept little or no market or price fluctuations and seeks low rates of returns to minimize risk.
(Money Market Fund)

---

2 http://www.seninvest.com/objectives.html

The general rule with retirement accounts is that the younger you are, the more aggressive your investment strategy can be. The reason is that even with market fluctuations, you will have time to recover and in the long term should increase the value of the money that you have invested. This rule of thumb works in the opposite direction as well. As you approach retirement you will want to move to a more conservative investment strategy looking at investment products and services that will carry a lower risk level. This is known as capital preservation or simply put – trying not to lose the money that you have earned and saved as you get closer to the time you plan to use it. As a young adult your money is going to be invested for at least a period of 40 plus years. With that in mind, **you can begin looking at mutual funds that have a moderate to aggressive risk level**.

Investment Category or Fund Classification

There are a variety of different types of mutual funds. There are *domestic stock funds, international funds, money market funds, index funds, bond funds, sector funds, target date funds* (balanced or asset allocation funds) and more. Within domestic stock funds you will see funds that may be categorized, depending on the mutual fund company, as large blend, large value, mid blend, mid growth, etc. With an aggressive risk level you can begin researching and analyzing domestic stock mutual funds that have a large growth or large cap growth *fund classification*.

These funds will focus on companies that are experiencing significant earnings or revenue growth. The companies will be commonly referred to as 'blue chip' companies, meaning they are the bellwether companies doing business. The hope is that these rapidly growing companies will continue to increase in value, thereby allowing the fund to reap the benefits of large capital gains. In general, growth funds are more volatile than other types of funds. Again the larger the chance for a higher return, the higher the risk level. But remember, we are matching the investment objective with the time horizon of over 40 – 50 years, giving you time to ride the potential market fluctuations of an aggressive mutual fund.

Growth Fund

When you look at **growth funds** you will see subsets of growth funds called *large-cap growth*, *mid-cap growth* and *small-cap growth*. We are going to be primarily concerned with funds that concentrate their assets in large-cap growth funds. To easily distinguish what each of these categories stand for you may use this rule of thumb; large-cap pertains to large companies with over $10 billion in market capitalization, mid-cap are medium sized companies with between $2 billion and $10 billion in market capitalization and small-cap are small companies with less than $2 billion in market capitalization. (Market capitalization is the total value of the outstanding shares for a company.)

You will also notice that the long established funds will have large asset balances from investors just like yourself. For example, Investment Company of America is a mutual fund established by American Funds. It has an inception (start) date of January 1, 1934. This particular mutual fund has been around for about 74 years. Over a 74 year period of time, this fund has been able to experience the ups and downs of various economic conditions. The experience is very impressive and along with that they have over three million shareholders and a net asset value of over $89 billion as of December 31, 2007.[3]

For the purpose of getting started you should focus your efforts on a growth fund. Then as you move forward in your life you will want to consider other types of fund classifications within your investment portfolio to create diversification. When you begin looking at other funds you will want to look at funds that do not have similar investment objectives, risk levels and especially duplicate companies.

Investment Objective

Once the fund classification is determined and you look at individual funds, another factor to further evaluate and analyze is the mutual fund's *investment objective*. These are the financial goals established for a

---

3 Annual report for the year ended December 31, 2007, American Funds Capital Research and Management Company.

specific mutual fund. Examples of investment objectives include the ability to generate long-term growth (typically for younger investors), capital preservation (typically for someone approaching retirement or investors trying to protect their money because of negative market conditions) or current income (typically for someone already in retirement or looking to supplement income). The objective is designed to achieve a certain desired outcome. It is important to narrow your choice to funds that have investment objectives that are in line with your personal investment goal(s). At your age, it is important that you look for investment objectives that feature growth or long term growth potential.

Growth mutual funds that have an aggressive investment objective will have a moderate to aggressive risk level or tolerance. The fund will be made up of primarily stocks as the major component of the fund (90-95%), with a small portion (5-10%) of other liquid assets (money market funds and bonds) that will round out the investment mix.

Performance

When you look at the vast array of mutual fund accounts and begin to narrow down your choices, you should be looking at the **fund's past performance**. The fund's performance will normally show the rate of return expressed as an annual percentage. This is called the *average annual total return*. This rate shows how the fund has performed and it will be expressed in increments such as 1 year, 3 years, 5 years, 10 years and from the inception date, the date the mutual fund originated. It is very common for people to get overly excited with the number that is the largest (which may be the 1 year number). However, you should concentrate on 10 years and over performance numbers. This will give you the proper indication of how this fund has performed over the many economic business fluctuations that have occurred in the world. A proven track record will enable you to analyze an account with the assurance that the mutual fund has been successful over time. You will hear and see it plenty when you begin investing: **past performance of a mutual fund will not guarantee future results**. Take the time to research mutual funds that have a sound financial history, it is your money, you are investing it and you need to have peace of mind.

Performance Evaluation

When evaluating the performance of a mutual fund there are two commonly used rating systems called *Morningstar* and the *Lipper Index*.

> **Morningstar** is an independent research firm that assists investors in identifying how a mutual fund compares against other funds of similar nature. The system is based upon a five star rating, 5 being excellent and 1 being poor. It was developed to assist individual investors in comparing and understanding their investments, specifically mutual funds. To research information visit their website at www.morningstar.com. For the purpose of this book you should look at only 4 or 5 star rated funds.
>
> **Lipper Index** analyzes mutual fund performance, as it relates to similar funds of its peers or sectors. The information that Lipper provides is called 'benchmarking,' with access to historical performance. Lipper provides over 85 indices. For further information visit www.lipperweb.com.

Net Asset Value

There are two ways that your mutual fund can increase in value, a rise in share value, and distributions from dividends and capital gains. First, when companies within the fund experience positive business performance the value for that stock increases (more people seek to buy the stock at a higher price) thus having a positive effect on the *Net Asset Value (NAV)* of the mutual fund. Second, when companies experience performance success they reward their shareholders with dividends (money from profits) that are then distributed to the mutual fund. Also, when the fund manager makes a decision to sell some of the shares, at a profit, of a particular stock that the fund holds, the capital gain (profit made from the sale of shares) is also distributed accordingly. This means the stocks were purchased at a lower price and sold for a higher price. It's what you always hope to do: **buy low and sell high**.

When you open a mutual fund account you will be given a choice how you would prefer to receive distributions. They can be paid to you directly (consult a tax advisor) however, to increase the balance of your account, you should *always* select **automatic reinvestment** for these distributions. This means that the earnings from dividend income and capital gain distributions will be automatically deposited to your account, and invested by acquiring more shares in the mutual fund. This is another way to take full advantage of the concept of compound interest.

Rule of 72

When comparing rates of return provided by the mutual fund there is a quick rule to help you project future earnings, called the Rule of 72. The *Rule of 72* is a simple way of determining the length of time it will take for your initial investment to double at a particular compounding *interest rate*.[4] You divide the number 72 by the interest rate that you are earning. So, for example if you want to know how long it is going to take for your money to double at the rate of 8%, you would divide 72 by 8 (72/8 = 9). It will take your money about nine years to double at that interest rate. This calculation provides you an *estimate* as a means of analyzing your ability to meet certain financial goals at certain dollar amounts and interest rates. It is a quick guideline to lend you insight on various investment strategies you are considering in meeting your financial goals. This calculation is often used by people who put off investing and are looking for ways to make up for lost time by being aggressive in their investment strategy. As we have discussed before, if you do not allow yourself sufficient time you are relying on the financial markets to be in your favor, which carries greater risk.

A basic table has been provided at the end of the chapter to give you an idea of how increases in interest rates, on a comparable basis, can make

---

4 http://www.investordictionary.com/definition/rule+of+72.aspx

a difference in the growth of your money. The table covers interest rates between 2% and 18% to show you how the interest rate has an overall impact on the earning potential and growth of your money. Remember, however, that the average rate of return of the Dow Jones Industrial Average over the last 111 years has been 5.3%.[5] Sustained rates of return in the higher percentages are extremely unlikely. The table is to be used just as a point of reference to look at and understand the power of the Rule of 72.

Major Indexes

You can also make comparisons with common stock market indexes that will indicate how well a specific mutual fund performs compared to other overall market conditions. Here are some common indexes:

Dow Jones Industrial Average
Standard and Poor's 500 (S&P 500)
NASDAQ

Dow Jones Industrial Average - The index is made up of 30 of the most actively traded blue chip stocks. It provides an indication of the overall condition of the United States stock market and is the most commonly used in reporting the day's overall performance. As market conditions and companies' performances change, the make up of the list can change. To see the current list of companies comprising the *Dow Jones Industrial Average* visit www.djindexes.com.

Standard and Poor's 500 (S&P 500) - An index that is made up of 500 stocks of major companies selected by market size, industry and liquidity and is market value weighted. The index provides an indication of the overall condition of the United States stock market and is commonly used in reporting

5http://www.djindexes.com/

the day's overall performance. The *S&P 500* is made up of 400 industrial firms, 40 financial firms, 20 transportation firms and 40 utilities. For a complete listing of the current companies listed in the S&P 500 visit www.standardandpoors.com.

NASDAQ (National Association of Securities Dealers Automated Quotations) - An electronic stock exchange that is made up of 3,300 companies. What makes the *NASDAQ* unique to the investment world is that it is an electronic exchange. Unlike the New York Stock Exchange, the NASDAQ has no trading floor, so it conducts all of its trading through computers and telecommunications equipment. In order to be a stock traded on the NASDAQ market, the company must meet certain base requirements including the price of the stock, which must be at least $1 and the value of outstanding stocks, which must be at least $1.1 million. Companies that are listed on the NASDAQ are primarily new, have high growth potential and can also be considered volatile. The NASDAQ conducts greater trading volume than any other stock exchange with nearly 1.8 billion trades a day. The NASDAQ provides an indication of the overall condition of a segment of the United States stock market and is commonly used in reporting the day's overall performance. For a complete listing of all the companies listed on the NASDAQ visit www.nasdaq.com.

Opening a Mutual Fund Account

When it comes to investing there are many choices in opening a mutual fund account. First, you can utilize your relationship with your bank and explore investment choices and options with mutual funds it offers. If you have a strong interest in a certain mutual fund company you can contact it directly to purchase a specific fund. You can contact a discount brokerage company such as Fidelity Investments, T. Rowe Price, Charles Schwab, etc. There are also *full service brokerage companies* such as Merrill Lynch & Co., Morgan Stanley, CitiBank Smith Barney, USB, Edward Jones, and Prudential, to name a few. Or, you can use an *insurance company* such as Northwestern Mutual, New York Life, The Principal Group, Allstate, The Hartford or John Hancock. Each source offers different products and services. To determine which is best for you, let's analyze the benefits and better understand the difference.

Sales Charge (Load & No Load) & Share Classes

When you select mutual funds you will have to decide if you are willing to pay a *sales charge (load)* or prefer a *no sales charge (no-load)* mutual fund to buy and sell shares. Front-end load is when a mutual fund has a sales charge for purchasing shares and back-end load (or a *deferred sales charge*) is when there is a sales charge for selling shares. Remember a front-end load will reduce the amount you are depositing, thus reducing the amount of your investment. This means you are investing less money. A back-end load will reduce the amount you are receiving. The amount of sales charge to be paid will be determined by the type of shares or class of shares that are purchased. There are three types of *share classes*, 'A,' 'B' or 'C.' The differentiation between the classes is that each one will have varied services, such as a front-load or back-end load, fees and expenses and/or distribution arrangements. There are a couple points to keep in mind. No matter what share class is purchased all monies invested will have the same investment objectives and policies of the fund. Also because of the different service fees that are offered each share class will have different performance results.

One may wonder then, "Why would you ever consider investing in a mutual fund that has a 'load' of any kind? Wouldn't it be in my best interest to stay clear of any investment that could potentially have a negative impact on my ability to save money?" In all fairness to the entire industry, there are reasons that one would invest in mutual funds that have a sales charge. You may have a strong preference to buy and own a particular fund. Many people want to own a specific fund because of certain attributes like a long standing history, successful past performances, and management expertise among other factors. Some mutual funds cannot be purchased without an investment advisor. If you want to purchase a fund that is only offered through an advisor, you must pay a sales charge.

The main advantage is turning over the selection process to an investment advisor or ***broker*** who has the expertise and training necessary to provide sound advice, specifically tailored to your personal investment situation. This person will be assisting you in planning your financial success. A financial advisor will:

- Provide advice and guidance in developing savings habits.

- Learn about your financial goals, understand your time horizon, and know your tolerance for risk.

- Assist in planning with a retirement savings calculation tool.

- Research and analyze various investments that would match your financial situation.

- Build a portfolio according to your financial goals.

- Monitor and review your account periodically.

Along with the selection and formation of a portfolio and the specific products and services to meet your financial goals, an investment advisor will also provide support and guidance including:

- Monitoring current market conditions.

- Recognizing how current financial problems effect overall market conditions.

- Understanding interest rate and/or currency fluctuations.

- Consulting, listening and being the voice of reason during stressful and demanding financial times.

An investment advisor's goal is to maximize the earning potential of an individual investor's portfolio, which is not guaranteed, but in theory will offset the sales charge incurred.

Each individual investor has their own investment objectives, goals and strategies. No one particular situation is considered better over another. Though the common advice may be to invest in a no-load mutual fund and have all of your invested dollars working for you, other conditions may exist that warrant alternate decisions. No matter what you choose the best advice is to – **be invested and stay invested – period.**

Discount Brokerage Company

We explored the reasons why someone may choose to pay a load when purchasing mutual funds, but we will now look at why the discount brokerage industry is so large and so successful. As the investment world has changed over the years one of the largest innovations has been the development of the discount brokerage industry. It has been able to single-handedly create the marketplace for the individual investor to become his/her own investment guru. It has allowed the individual investor to be able to take full control and responsibility of his/her investment decisions. And with technological advances, and companies that provide investor assistance, the individual investor can create, as well as alter a portfolio to his/her liking.

The individual investor now has the ability to create diversified portfolios using mutual funds and a vast array of other investment vehicles, along with acting as a stockbroker delving into more sophisticated and advanced activities, including trading stocks, which used to be the privilege of only a *stockbroker*.

Discount brokerage companies offer a full array of investment products and services, similar to that of a full service brokerage company with one major difference, no sales charges on mutual fund purchases. Major discount brokerage companies include Fidelity Investments, T. Rowe Price, Charles Schwab, and Scottrade to name a few.

With a discount brokerage company you will be directly

responsible for managing your portfolio, and managing the specific decision making process in creating your portfolio. In essence you will be the stockbroker, the fund manager in a sense, because you will be the one creating the diversification of the funds and investments that you choose. When you begin working with a discount brokerage service, you will have access to excellent customer service and investment advisors that will be able to assist you with answering your questions regarding individual products and services. But in the end, it will be you who will be the final decision maker, giving specific instructions to be carried out.

With the advancement of technology and the abundance of information that is available to an investor online, it is totally possible for someone, like yourself, to learn, understand and teach yourself how to make successful investment choices and decisions. *Start early*, take responsibility for your financial future and create a path to building financial wealth. Yes, it can be done by doing it yourself.

One of the biggest advantages of using a discount brokerage company is the cost of doing business. This is never more evident than by analyzing the mutual fund offerings that are available on a 'no load' basis. What this means is that *every dollar* invested is being deposited to your account to begin working for you and earning interest. That is not the only feature that makes them attractive, because the same benefits of a full service brokerage company's mutual fund can also be enjoyed by using a discount brokerage company. Mutual funds from a discount brokerage company will also have top rated Morningstar and Lipper Index funds that are handled by professional fund managers acting on your behalf to successfully achieve the fund's goals and objectives. They will offer a variety of funds that can be used to create a successful, diversified portfolio so you may practice 'not placing all your eggs in one basket,' a key to successful investing.

Without the services of an investment advisor you will have to monitor current market conditions and pay attention to interest rate and currency fluctuations as noted previously. You will also need to learn how to use a retirement savings calculator to assist you in determining the desired savings needed for retirement. In addition to those duties you will have to practice patience and continue to learn and understand your personal financial situation and make investment decisions and adjustments, when needed, independently.

Fees

A mutual fund is no different than any other type of business that offers products and services. There are certain costs and *fees* associated with doing business and owning a mutual fund. These fees are separate from incurring a sales charge for purchasing and selling shares, and are associated with all mutual funds. When analyzing mutual fund accounts, please take the time to learn and understand the importance of being able to **properly compare the fees** that are associated with the fund. They can vary and ultimately have an effect on the overall rate of return of the fund over the years. Higher fees or expenses associated with the account will increase the impact they have on the overall performance of the account over its life.

Expenses or fees associated with mutual fund accounts will vary from fund to fund. There can be *account fees* for maintenance of an account. These fees may be charged separately to your account. There will be a *management fee* for a fund or portfolio manager managing the fund and drawing upon his/her expertise to meet the fund's objectives. One of the most common fees in comparing mutual funds is the *distribution* [and/or service] *fees* ('12b-1' fees). These are the fees associated with a mutual fund that include the marketing and selling of shares, advertising, sales literature, compensation for brokers and printing and mailing of literature.

Lastly, you should consider the *total annual fund operating expenses* (*expense ratio*). This is the total of all expenses associated with a mutual fund. Many are subtracted from the overall fund's assets and will affect the annual rate of return associated with the fund. There are mutual fund cost calculation tools available online that can assist you in computing the costs of different mutual funds and how it can affect your overall earnings. A complete description of a mutual fund's fees and additional information regarding the specifics of a mutual fund will be disclosed in the fund's prospectus.

Minimum Balance Requirement

When establishing a mutual fund account you will be **required to open the account with a minimum balance**. Depending on the type of account, either a regular mutual fund account or an IRA, the minimum balance requirement can vary from $100 to $2,500. There will also be certain factors, such as setting up an *automatic investment plan* (which is when money is automatically transferred to the account on a regular basis) which may reduce the minimum balance required.

Prospectus

After researching, analyzing and evaluating the type of mutual fund that seems right for you, you will now request or download a *prospectus*. Contrary to what it may seem, *prospectus* was not the ancient Greek philosopher of investing. A prospectus is an official document produced by a mutual fund company describing in detail the specifics of a mutual fund to prospective investors including:

- Name of the fund and ticker symbol

- Investment objective of the fund

- Strategies used for meeting the objectives outlined

- Risk level of the fund

- Past performance of the fund, this information will normally be displayed in two forms, a bar chart and a table with return information listed

- Fees and expenses associated with the fund

- Share pricing policies

- How to buy and sell shares

- Distribution and tax information

- Qualifications and background of the fund manager responsible for the performance of the fund, as it relates to the objectives and strategies

- General investing information including how to open an account, information about services, customer service contact information, etc.

You should obtain this important information in order to make sure that a specific mutual fund is the right fit and meets your goals and objectives. All investment companies that offer mutual funds are required by the SEC (the Securities and Exchange Commission), to issue a prospectus.

It is imperative that you request a prospectus from the specific mutual fund companies that you are considering. NEVER make an investment decision without reading the prospectus. Remember, this is your hard earned money, you need to invest it in a wise, informed and practical manner.

Along with a prospectus, it can also be helpful and educational to order or download the most recent **quarterly report or annual report**. These reports will contain more recent information on how the fund is performing and also explain how the current stock market conditions have been affecting the activity and performance of the fund. It will also contain very detailed information about the industry holdings within the portfolio of investments in each business sector. This is an excellent way to gain a clear understanding of the investment objectives that will assist you in both evaluating and choosing a mutual fund.

Other Information

Other than the assistance of an investment advisor, there are plenty of investment tools, including mutual fund cost calculators, available through various financial institution websites, which can assist you in properly comparing, to make the best educated decision. Here are just a few of the web based services that can be used to conduct research and compare mutual funds:

MarketWatch	www.marketwatch.com/tools/mutualfunds/
Smart Money	www.smartmoney.com/fundanalyzer
SEC	www.sec.gov/investor/tools/mfcc/mfcc-int.html
FINRA	http://apps.finra.org/Investor_Information/ EA/1/mfetf.aspx

After you establish a mutual fund account you will regularly receive large amounts of information regarding your account, as well as other financial information for you to review and consider. These documents will help you monitor and review your account:

Quarterly Statements - this will summarize all the activity that has transpired within your account over the past 90 days. It will state such things as purchase dates of shares, number of shares and value of your account. When you receive it, review it in detail and if there is anything you do not understand, contact your mutual fund company or investment advisor to learn more.

Semi-Annual and Annual Reports - detailed reports about the overall fund performance as a whole, for all shareholders. These reports come within 60 days after the end of the middle of the year and the end of the fiscal year. When you receive it, review it in detail and if there is anything you do not understand, contact your mutual fund company or investment advisor.

These important points from the *Securities and Exchange Commission* (also known as the SEC) are also very valuable and pertinent:

> Mutual fund accounts **will not be guaranteed**. They will not be insured by any insurance company or government agency, like the FDIC (Federal Deposit Insurance Corporation) which insures certain bank accounts.
>
> A mutual fund is an investment product and does carry risk. You can lose money by investing in mutual funds.

FINRA

It is common place today to pick up a newspaper, watch the evening news or see on a business program numerous stories relating to the business world, and in particular investment practices of individuals and companies alike. It is disturbing to hear about individuals that fall prey to the deceptive practices of those who thrive on taking advantage of others. Despite giving the appearance that they have others' best interest at heart in investing their money and making it grow, these individuals outright steal the investors' hard earned money that they planned to live on later in life.

This is when people always seem to say, "I don't know what to do" or, "I don't know whom to contact." It is important to know that there is an agency out there to help you if you ever feel that you have a problem. *FINRA (Financial Industry Regulatory Authority)*, is the largest non-governmental regulator for all securities firms doing business in the United States. FINRA is there to assist in protecting investors from falling prey to deceitful and unlawful investment practices and with situations that they feel have been mishandled or are deceptive. With FINRA, investors can file a complaint, even with law abiding, upstanding investment companies or investment professionals. Very simply put, **this agency is on your side; it is a trusted advocate for investors and is concerned with the overall**

protection of peoples' hard earned money.

It is possible that you may never have to contact FINRA; hopefully not. But it is important as you plan for your financial future and become an investor that you know there is someone out there that can help you in case you encounter a problem. For more information visit the FINRA website at www.finra.org/index.html. Become familiar with all they have for the individual investor. You will find that they also offer a variety of services to assist you in their Education and Programs section.

You are probably wondering, is this section ever going to end? I know the length of it is by far longer and more involved than anything we have discussed up until this point, but this program is designed to place a heavy emphasis on helping you develop sound personal money management skills and habits with the ultimate goal of beginning to save for your retirement. Establishing a mutual fund account, along with a savings account, is critical to your financial future and there is much to learn to make wise choices. There are varieties of mutual funds available, as well as much information about the make up of a mutual fund account and I have tried to break it down in the most basic form. It may seem like it is a lot of information, but it is just the beginning of what you will learn as you become more involved with your account and you develop a further understanding of investing as you become older.

You have done a great job getting through all this information; it is really important that you know and understand what was discussed. I wish you the best of luck as you now research and choose the mutual fund that you feel is the best for you to establish your investment portfolio. Whew! Great job, let's move on.

Appendix - Rule of 72 Table

Rule of 72 Interest Rate	No. of Yrs.	
1%	72.0	
2%	36.0	Typical Savings Account
3%	24.0	
4%	18.0	
5%	14.4	
6%	12.0	Typical Mutual Fund
7%	10.3	Investment
8%	9.0	
9%	8.0	
10%	7.2	
11%	6.5	
12%	6.0	High Risk Investments
13%	5.5	
14%	5.1	
15%	4.8	
16%	4.5	
17%	4.2	Unrealistic Expectations
18%	4.0	

Chapter 10

MAXIMIZE YOUR EARNING POWER

Y ou know you need to save, and you have learned about savings accounts and mutual funds – now what? Let's look at investment strategies and your account options so that you can maximize your earning power.

Type of Account

When you have determined the large cap growth fund that best meets your investment objectives there are three ways to invest your money. First, there is a straight mutual fund in which you open an account and begin making contributions. This is the type of account you will open if you are not working and do not have earned income. If you are working, earning income and receiving a W-2 you can take advantage of significant tax benefits by opening an *Individual Retirement Account (IRA)*. There are two types of IRA accounts, a traditional IRA and a Roth IRA.

The traditional IRA is a tax deferred account in which you will invest pre-taxed dollars and pay taxes on the contributions and earnings when it is withdrawn in retirement. Though the traditional IRA may benefit some older Americans, the Roth is by far the best choice for young adults.

Roth IRA

The *Roth IRA* is a great investment vehicle to begin with. The reason for its popularity is that while you invest with taxed dollars up front, all earnings are tax free. Because you are young and pay taxes in what should be a lower tax bracket now than when you retire, this is a significant tax advantage to you. When you begin to withdraw the funds, the money will not be taxed and you will owe nothing. The other key advantages over a traditional IRA include avoiding penalties for early withdrawal of the initially invested money, as well as avoiding a minimum distribution requirement from the account after age 70 ½. Upon retirement, if you have other retirement accounts that will provide income you can continue to leave the money invested in your Roth IRA to grow and earn even more interest.

To qualify for a Roth IRA, you will have to meet minimum eligibility requirements. The requirements are:

> - You need to have qualified earned income from a job.
> - You can only save what you earn, up to a maximum of $4,000 in 2009 (This is one of those times, again, to seek the expertise of a tax professional.)

The benefits of owning a Roth IRA don't stop there. There are some additional features that make this a viable investment choice:

Penalty Free Withdrawals - Despite being able to utilize the Roth IRA as an investment account for retirement, you may also be able to make withdrawals of your contributions, not your earnings, **any time, tax free** and the biggest advantage is **without a penalty** that other IRA accounts have. However, if you withdraw the earnings on the account prior to the age of 59 ½ you will incur tax consequences and penalties. Remember, we are developing sound money management skills with an emphasis on saving money for retirement. The thought of **withdrawing this money for an emergency, as much as it is a 'benefit,' should never be a substitute for a properly planned emergency fund**.

Home Buying - The IRS will also allow you to withdraw from a Roth IRA contributions *and earnings*, tax free, for you to purchase a home. There is a $10,000 limit and the account has to be open a minimum of five years.

The way this account has been designed is really a no-brainer for a young adult to consider in establishing an investment portfolio, even if they are participating in a company 401(k) program. There are specific rules and regulations that govern a Roth IRA, as well as other IRAs, so consult a financial representative, investment professional or a tax professional to assist you with this matter.

Dollar Cost Averaging

In continuing to stress the importance of saving money on a regular, periodic basis, let's look at an investment strategy that will both reinforce the habit of systematically saving money and, at the same time, fully complement the building of an investment portfolio.

The habit is called *Dollar Cost Averaging* (DCA). It reinforces the habit of saving on a prescribed periodic basis and is a very important and proven financial concept in developing a solid financial investment portfolio. This falls right in line with the important habit of budgeting and is very similar in its working. Coupled with the Roth IRA, dollar cost averaging is a good decision when it comes to establishing an investment strategy and portfolio for young adults.

Dollar cost averaging means that you will invest a fixed dollar amount in the mutual fund on a regular basis for a long period of time. By doing so, you should be able to reduce your average share cost because you are reducing your risk of purchasing a greater amount of shares in the fund when the *Net Asset Value (NAV)* is higher. This works hand in hand with establishing a budget and consistently setting aside 10% of your money for retirement. It is called dollar cost averaging because over a period of time the cost of shares are averaged as they are being purchased at different NAV amounts due to market fluctuation.

With dollar cost averaging, you will be able to eliminate a very dangerous habit that a lot of people like to practice, trying to '**time the market**.' This means you are trying to 'estimate or guess' when you think that certain stock market conditions will exist that will allow you to invest a sum of money when prices are at their lowest point. In the history of Wall Street there is no way that anyone has been able to consistently or accurately predict the opportune time to purchase an investment or time the market. If it happens, trust me, it is based more on luck and chance than skill. The major problem when you do this is that you are trying to predict market conditions. If you are on the sidelines, not investing your money, and the market does not go lower but actually keeps going higher and higher, you have now just missed out on the increase in market value for your investment. When you do finally jump in you are purchasing at a higher share cost, thus purchasing less shares than if you would have utilized dollar cost averaging. As a result of trying to time the market, you have now purchased fewer shares. Utilizing dollar cost averaging is essential to building a financial portfolio over time. Get into the habit of doing it; it is one of the most under utilized and misunderstood financial concepts.

Dollar Cost Averaging Case Study

To reinforce just how important the investment strategy of dollar cost averaging is, let's look at an example of two investors. Both investors want to invest $600.00. Investor #1, Ella, is a practical investor and is reading a life changing financial book by Mr. Wagner. She decides to heed the advice and chooses to utilize dollar cost averaging. By doing so, Ella invests $100.00 per month for six months. Investor #2, Richard, is a self-proclaimed stock market guru. He is the guy walking around at a party, hiking up his pants and bragging about how great his investment choices are. No matter what the market is doing – he is, "totally out pacing it." Richard chooses to 'time' the market, investing the entire $600.00, in one lump sum, on March 15th.

In reviewing the investment scenarios and the strategies associated with both investors, they have different outcomes. Ella, using dollar cost averaging, was able to accumulate a total of 33.20 shares. Investment guru Richard, while trying to time the market, jumped in on March 15th and accumulated 30 shares. At the end of the six months, Ella acquired an additional 3.20 shares over Richard and achieved an ending account balance of $630.80 or $60.80 more than the 'guru.'

	Ella --DCA			'Guru' Richard --Lump Sum		
Date	NAV Share Price	# of Shares	Cost	NAV Share Price	# of Shares	Cost
1/15	$21	4.76	$100.00			
2/15	$19	5.26	$100.00			
3/15	$20	5.00	$100.00	$20	30.00	$600.00
4/15	$15	6.67	$100.00			
5/15	$16	6.25	$100.00			
6/15	$19	5.26	$100.00			
		33.20	$600.00		30.00	$600.00
Average Price per Share			$ 18.07			$ 20.00
Total fund value on 6/15			$630.80*			$570.00*
Gain/(Loss)			$ 30.80			($ 30.00)

*Note: The total fund value has been calculated based upon the NAV share price at the close of the market on 6/15. The total value, for example purposes only, does not take into consideration any dividends or capital gains that may affect the total fund value.

As basic as the example is, when you review the two investors, it demonstrates how effective dollar cost averaging can be, especially when practiced over the long term. As we have discussed, it is imperative that you take advantage of the precious commodity of time – because when you combine it with dollar cost averaging it can lead to developing both the habit and ability to increase the amount of shares you will own over time. In the example used, in only a six month period of time Ella's portfolio grew by 3.20 shares over the guru's. You can only imagine how the 'guru' is spinning his story, "If I'd only waited one more month…." Coulda, shoulda, woulda. Blah, blah, blah. It cannot be guaranteed, but if you are disciplined and use persistence and perseverance (which are good traits to use in other areas of your life) you will increase your chances of creating a solid financial future.

You can only reap the benefits of building a successful investment portfolio – taking advantage of the stock market as it relates to your investment accounts – if you are invested. If there is only one thing you take away from this section it is just that, **to be invested you need to stay invested**. At this early stage in your life you can take full advantage of having time on your side. By combining all four of the important financial ingredients, planning, budgeting, dollar cost averaging and time you will not just develop excellent personal money management skills, but you will establish the foundation needed to maximize your earning power.

I know you may be thinking that there is so much information to retain and understand, but you have done a great job and remember that the benefits of taking the time now to understand it will enable you to reap huge rewards from your hard work. Let's move on.

Chapter 11

THE TWO-HEADED MONSTER

U p until this point we have been discussing, in detail, the importance of saving while emphasizing the development of good, sound financial habits that will benefit you in your life. We discussed the process of budgeting and the importance of establishing separate accounts including a retirement savings account, a regular savings account, a giving or charity account and an emergency fund. We've stressed the importance of continually setting money aside, on a monthly basis, in each of these accounts with an understanding that there will be a need to utilize each of them, some now and some in the future. We have also touched upon resisting the temptation of purchasing items on credit.

Part I – The Head With the Smiling Face

Now that you have gained an understanding of the habits that are necessary to build a financial future, how does it really work? How does it to pay off in the long run? There is one more critical element that needs to be discussed and understood. This will make it perfectly clear why time, persistence and patience are so important in establishing a path to your financial future.

Compound Interest

'The Two-Headed Monster' is about exploring one common financial reality that works in opposite directions. This is called *compound interest*. The true definition of compound interest is, "interest upon interest, where accrued interest is added to the principal sum and the whole is treated as new principal, for the calculation of the interest for the next period." [1] In a simplified manner, the money that you are earning on your investment is being added to the balance of the account and interest is then earned on the new balance, including the interest that was previously added. Like the definition stated, interest upon interest – which means **making money while you sleep**. The magic happens when the interest is paid upon interest and is duplicated over and over and over again; your money grows and increases in value and the longer the time period that you allow your money to do this, the greater accumulation you will have. This is why you are reading this book, right? To create opportunities that will allow you to save and earn as much money as you can, so that you can live comfortably later in life and possibly not need to continue to work as long because of the financial decisions that you can make in your life right now.

I can see the dollar signs in your eyes and I can hear the 'cha ching, cha ching' of the cash register as you envision the money multiplying in your account and the balance getting bigger and bigger. You look like the mad laboratory scientist in one of those old black and white thriller movies, rubbing your hands feverishly, and screaming, "ha-ha, ha-ha, and ha-ha, it's alive." But wait, snap out of your moment of temporary insanity and come back to reality for a moment. Not to spoil this great and exciting moment for you but I have to splash cold water across your face. Pssssst, there is a small secret I need to let you in on about compound interest. Remember the title of this section, 'The Two-Headed Monster?' Well, this is the little secret. Compound interest is a two-headed monster. Why? It all sounds

---

1 http://www.investordictionary.com/definition/compound+interest.aspx

great and it can be, but at the same time it can also be damaging. How can something be so great one moment and be so bad the next moment? Well, just as you can earn more money from compound interest, you can lose it at the same time when you make foolish financial decisions by burying yourself in debt. Because when you are in debt you are going to be paying interest to a financial entity that has lent you money. When you borrow money from them that you don't have now, you must pay them back with interest added. See, you can 'earn' interest, which is a good thing, or 'pay' interest which is sometimes a very bad thing. There are going to be times when you will pay interest that is necessary, like when you borrow money for a car or buying a home. But just because you have to pay interest, there is nothing that says you have to pay it unnecessarily for a long time. When you understand the dual concept of interest, you will be able to effectively manage both situations and ultimately benefit from it to its fullest.

The most compelling way to demonstrate the power of compounding interest is by comparing various types of investors. It should ALWAYS be noted that there are risks in investing and that nothing is guaranteed. Remember, PAST RESULTS DO NOT GUARANTEE FUTURE PERFORMANCE. But also remember that the stock market has been in operation for over 111 years. There is plenty of history on your side. Let's take a look at each case.

Investor Case Studies

Utilizing multiple investor scenarios and corresponding tables will best demonstrate the power of compounding interest.[2] The scenarios will include using Dollar Cost Averaging at different stages in life. For the purpose of the examples a common retirement age of 62 has been used.

---

2 http://www.banksite.com/calc/savings (savings tables)

Investor #1 Begins at age 23

Year	Age	Per Month	Per Year	Ending Balance Including Interest
1	23	100	$1,200	$ 1,245
2	24	100	$1,200	$ 2,594
3	25	100	$1,200	$ 4,055
4	26	100	$1,200	$ 7,353
5	27	100	$1,200	$ 7,204
6	28	100	$1,200	$ 9,210
7	29	100	$1,200	$ 11,222
8	30	100	$1,200	$ 13,402
9	31	100	$1,200	$ 15,763
10	32	100	$1,200	$ 18,321
11	33	(0)	(0)	$ 19,847
12	34	(0)	(0)	$ 21,500
13	35	(0)	(0)	$ 23,290
14	36	(0)	(0)	$ 25,230
15	37	(0)	(0)	$ 27,331
16	38	(0)	(0)	$ 29,607
17	39	(0)	(0)	$ 32,073
18	40	(0)	(0)	$ 34,743
19	41	(0)	(0)	$ 37,636
20	42	(0)	(0)	$ 40,771
21	43	(0)	(0)	$ 44,166
22	44	(0)	(0)	$ 47,844
23	45	(0)	(0)	$ 51,828
24	46	(0)	(0)	$ 56,144
25	47	(0)	(0)	$ 60,820
26	48	(0)	(0)	$ 65,885
27	49	(0)	(0)	$ 71,371
28	50	(0)	(0)	$ 77,315
29	51	(0)	(0)	$ 83,754
30	52	(0)	(0)	$ 90,728
31	53	(0)	(0)	$ 98,284
32	54	(0)	(0)	$106,469
33	55	(0)	(0)	$115,335
34	56	(0)	(0)	$124,940
35	57	(0)	(0)	$135,345
36	58	(0)	(0)	$146,616
37	59	(0)	(0)	$158,826
38	60	(0)	(0)	$172,052
39	61	(0)	(0)	$186,380
40	62	(0)	(0)	**$201,902**

Total invested	$ 12,000
Total invested with the interest earned up until year 11	$ 18,321
Total interest earned @ 8% annual rate of return	$183,581
Total savings balance in the account	**$201,902**

In this scenario, Investor #1 began investing at the age of 23. The investor deposited $100 each month into his/her account on a consistent basis for 10 years. After the final deposit into the account at the end of year 10 the investor stopped saving. The investor let the money remain in the account for the next 30 years, depositing no further monies. Utilizing the average rate of return of 8%, the total account balance at the end of the 40 years would be approximately $201,902.

Investor #2 Begins at age 33

Year	Age	Per Month	Per Year	Ending Balance Including Interest
1	33	100	$1,200	$ 1,245
2	34	100	$1,200	$ 2,594
3	35	100	$1,200	$ 4,055
4	36	100	$1,200	$ 5,638
5	37	100	$1,200	$ 7,353
6	38	100	$1,200	$ 9,210
7	39	100	$1,200	$ 11,222
8	40	100	$1,200	$ 13,402
9	41	100	$1,200	$ 15,763
10	42	100	$1,200	$ 18,321
11	43	100	$1,200	$ 21,092
12	44	100	$1,200	$ 24,094
13	45	100	$1,200	$ 27,345
14	46	100	$1,200	$ 30,867
15	47	100	$1,200	$ 34,683
16	48	100	$1,200	$ 38,817
17	49	100	$1,200	$ 43,294
18	50	100	$1,200	$ 48,145
19	51	100	$1,200	$ 53,399
20	52	100	$1,200	$ 59,091
21	53	100	$1,200	$ 65,258
22	54	100	$1,200	$ 71,937
23	55	100	$1,200	$ 79,173
24	56	100	$1,200	$ 87,012
25	57	100	$1,200	$ 95,503
26	58	100	$1,200	$104,701
27	59	100	$1,200	$114,666
28	60	100	$1,200	$125,460
29	61	100	$1,200	$137,153
30	62	100	$1,200	**$149,820**

Total invested	$ 36,000
Total interest earned @ 8% annual rate of return	$113,820
Total savings balance in the account	**$149,820**

In this scenario, Investor #2 put off saving for 10 years and begins investing at the age of 33. The investor deposited $100 each month into his/her account on a consistent basis for 30 years. Utilizing the average rate of return of 8%, the total account balance at the end of the 30 years would be approximately $149,820.

In looking at the comparisons between Investor #1 & #2, Investor #2 ended up investing an additional $24,000 more than Investor #1. What is so compelling about this comparison is that even though Investor #2 invested the additional $24,000, the overall balance of the portfolio was significantly less than Investor #1, by $52,082. Investor #1 only invested $12,000, or one-third the amount, and earned a lot more.

Investor #3 Begins at age 23

Year	Age	Per Month	Per Year	Ending Balance Including Interest
1	23	100	$1,200	$ 1,245
2	24	100	$1,200	$ 2,594
3	25	100	$1,200	$ 4,055
4	26	100	$1,200	$ 5,638
5	27	100	$1,200	$ 7,353
6	28	100	$1,200	$ 9,210
7	29	100	$1,200	$ 11,222
8	30	100	$1,200	$ 13,402
9	31	100	$1,200	$ 15,763
10	32	100	$1,200	$ 18,321
11	33	100	$1,200	$ 21,092
12	34	100	$1,200	$ 24,094
13	35	100	$1,200	$ 27,345
14	36	100	$1,200	$ 30,867
15	37	100	$1,200	$ 34,683
16	38	100	$1,200	$ 38,817
17	39	100	$1,200	$ 43,294
18	40	100	$1,200	$ 48,145
19	41	100	$1,200	$ 53,399
20	42	100	$1,200	$ 59,091
21	43	100	$1,200	$ 65,258
22	44	100	$1,200	$ 71,937
23	45	100	$1,200	$ 79,173
24	46	100	$1,200	$ 87,012
25	47	100	$1,200	$ 95,503
26	48	100	$1,200	$104,701
27	49	100	$1,200	$114,666
28	50	100	$1,200	$125,460
29	51	100	$1,200	$137,153

Investor #3, cont.

30	52	100	$1,200	$149,820
31	53	100	$1,200	$163,541
32	54	100	$1,200	$178,406
33	55	100	$1,200	$194,508
34	56	100	$1,200	$211,952
35	57	100	$1,200	$230,848
36	58	100	$1,200	$251,317
37	59	100	$1,200	$273,491
38	60	100	$1,200	$297,512
39	61	100	$1,200	$323,533
40	62	100	$1,200	**$351,722**

Total invested	$ 48,000
Total interest earned @ 8% annual rate of return	$303,722
Total savings balance in the account	**$351,722**

In this scenario, Investor #3 decided to begin investing at the age of 23. The investor deposited $100 each month into his/her account on a consistent basis for 40 years. Utilizing the average rate of return of 8%, the total account balance at the end of the 40 years would be approximately $351,722.

When looking at the comparisons between Investor #2 & #3, Investor #3 invested an additional $12,000 more than Investor #2. But as a result of compound interest and Investor #3 beginning earlier, it had a life changing effect on the portfolio balance of Investor #3, a staggering $201,902 more for retirement. When you make financial decisions throughout your life that have those kinds of monetary ramifications, it can have a significant impact on how you will live your life in the future. When you begin talking about decisions that effect your life by six-figures, those are serious decisions; you are playing with a lot of money.

Investor #4 Begins at age 43

Year	Age	Per Month	Per Year	Ending Balance Including Interest
1	43	100	$1,200	$1,245
2	44	100	$1,200	$2,594
3	45	100	$1,200	$4,055
4	46	100	$1,200	$5,638
5	47	100	$1,200	$7,353
6	48	100	$1,200	$9,210

Investor #4, cont.

7	49	100	$1,200	$11,222
8	50	100	$1,200	$13,402
9	51	100	$1,200	$15,763
10	52	100	$1,200	$18,321
11	53	100	$1,200	$21,092
12	54	100	$1,200	$24,094
13	55	100	$1,200	$27,345
14	56	100	$1,200	$30,867
15	57	100	$1,200	$34,683
16	58	100	$1,200	$38,817
17	59	100	$1,200	$43,294
18	60	100	$1,200	$48,145
19	61	100	$1,200	$53,399
20	62	100	$1,200	**$59,091**

Total invested	$24,000
Total interest earned @ 8% annual rate of return	$35,091
Total savings balance in the account	**$59,091**

In this scenario, Investor #4 put off saving for 20 years and decided to begin investing at the age of 43. The investor deposited $100 each month into his/her account on a consistent basis for 20 years. Utilizing the average rate of return of 8%, the total account balance at the end of the 20 years would be approximately $59,091.

Now that we have looked at the scenarios and made some comparisons with the power of compounding interest and taking advantage of time, let's talk about how costly the mistake of putting off saving until a later date can be. Investor #4 waited an additional ten years from Investor #2 and began investing at the age of 43. Keeping the retirement age as the same, 62, Investor #4 was only able to put away $24,000 in 20 years and established a final savings balance of $59,091. When you look at this number, compared to all the other investor scenarios that we have looked at, you will probably say, "Why would I do that?" Well, believe it or not, there are a lot of people out there today that are in this position or even worse. But, as we have discussed previously, there are life situations that can and will occur that can detour you from your financial path and will significantly impact your ability to properly plan and save. That is why we talk about getting started EARLY in your life, before some of those life situations occur. There are going to be temptations that can interfere, there will be credit cards that you want to use, houses you want to buy, a life that you want to live but may not be able to afford, employment or unemployment issues that arise; you get the point. By putting things off and making some unfortunate decisions you will put yourself in a similar position to that of Investor #4.

Another thing that happens that affects the decision making process is waiting and saying you will do it later, planning to catch up by investing more money. Well, as easy as that may sound, it isn't. Let's look at that scenario with Investor #4-W, for waiting.

Investor #4-W Begins at age 43

Year	Age	Per Month	Per Year	Ending Balance Including Interest
1	43	595.22	$7,142.64	$ 8,056
2	44	595.22	$7,142.64	$ 15,440
3	45	595.22	$7,142.64	$ 24,137
4	46	595.22	$7,142.64	$ 33,558
5	47	595.22	$7,142.64	$ 43,764
6	48	595.22	$7,142.64	$ 54,820
7	49	595.22	$7,142.64	$ 66,797
8	50	595.22	$7,142.64	$ 79,771
9	51	595.22	$7,142.64	$ 93,825
10	52	595.22	$7,142.64	$109,050
11	53	595.22	$7,142.64	$125,543
12	54	595.22	$7,142.64	$143,409
13	55	595.22	$7,142.64	$162,763
14	56	595.22	$7,142.64	$183,729
15	57	595.22	$7,142.64	$206,441
16	58	595.22	$7,142.64	$231,044
17	59	595.22	$7,142.64	$257,696
18	60	595.22	$7,142.64	$286,568
19	61	595.22	$7,142.64	$317,844
20	62	595.22	$7,142.64	**$351,724**

Total invested	$142,853
Total interest earned @ 8% annual rate of return	$208,871
Total savings balance in the account	**$351,724**

In this scenario, Investor #4-W put off saving for over 20 years and decided to begin investing at the age of 43. The difference with Investor #4-W is that he/she wanted to accumulate a similar account balance value as Investor #3 or approximately $355,722. In order to 'catch up' Investor #4-W would have to deposit $595.22 each month into his/her account on a consistent basis for 20 years. Utilizing the average rate of return of 8%, the total account balance at the end of the 20 years would be approximately $351,724.

Investor Scenario Comparison Chart 1

	Total Money Invested	Length of Investment	Length of Growth (years)	Ending Balance
Investor #1				
	$12,000	10	40	$201,902
Investor #2				
	$36,000	30	30	$149,820
Investor #3				
	$48,000	40	40	$351,722
Investor #4				
	$24,000	20	20	$ 59,091
Investor #4-W				
	$142,853	20	20	$351,724

It is best to compare apples to apples, using a fair quantitative comparison. Looking back, Investor #3 began investing at the age 23 and chose to consistently invest $100 per month for 40 years. At the age of 62 the account had grown from the $48,000 invested over the time to around $351,722, assuming the average rate of return was 8%. Investor #4-W wanted to arrive at the same savings balance, however only had 20 years to do it. In order to have achieved a balance of about $350,000 at age 62 Investor #4-W would have to start investing approximately $595.22 per month, (almost 6 times more, per month, than Investor #3) or $7,142.64 per year. Investor #4-W would also have to maintain the discipline to continue to invest that amount monthly for the next 20 years. At the end of that time period the total amount invested would be $142,853. That's a high price to pay for waiting and making up for lost time. To break it down in simpler terms. Investor #4-W, would end up investing an additional

$94,853 to establish a savings balance equal to what Investor #3 did with only $48,000, having to invest almost triple the amount of money to end up with about the same amount. Now you can see the extreme financial ramifications and how costly that decision can be.

There is one other thing to consider. When you look at Investor #3, he/she has taken advantage of over 47 years of stock market performance in both positive and negative economic conditions. With Investor #4-W, riding the ups and downs of the stock market over only 20 years is an additional risk with less time for the stock market to regain its momentum, if needed. This could significantly alter the overall annual rate of return and the financial outcome of the account. The examples use an 8% average rate of return, which is a fairly commonly used figure when calculating this type of information. Remember the average rate of return of the Dow Jones Industrial Average over that past 111 years (since its inception) has been 5.30%.[3] That is why it is so important to allow yourself as much time as possible to take advantage of more positive market conditions and have time to ride the wave of less favorable market conditions.

The next comparison is one of the reasons that drives my passion to bring this program to young adults. This scenario will establish how the combination of planning, budgeting, dollar cost averaging, compound interest and time can significantly impact the results.

Investor #5 Begins at age 16

Year	Age	Per Month	Per Year	Ending Balance Including Interest
1	16	100	$1,200	$ 1,245
2	17	100	$1,200	$ 2,594
3	18	100	$1,200	$ 4,055
4	19	100	$1,200	$ 7,353
5	20	100	$1,200	$ 7,204
6	21	100	$1,200	$ 9,210
7	22	100	$1,200	$ 11,222
8	23	100	$1,200	$ 13,402
9	24	100	$1,200	$ 15,763
10	25	100	$1,200	$ 18,321
11	26	(0)	(0)	$ 19,847
12	27	(0)	(0)	$ 21,500

3 http://www.djindexes.com/

Investor #5, cont.

13	28	(0)	(0)	$ 23,290
14	29	(0)	(0)	$ 25,230
15	30	(0)	(0)	$ 27,331
16	31	(0)	(0)	$ 29,607
17	32	(0)	(0)	$ 32,073
18	33	(0)	(0)	$ 34,743
19	34	(0)	(0)	$ 37,636
20	35	(0)	(0)	$ 40,771
21	36	(0)	(0)	$ 44,166
22	37	(0)	(0)	$ 47,844
23	38	(0)	(0)	$ 51,828
24	39	(0)	(0)	$ 56,144
25	40	(0)	(0)	$ 60,820
26	41	(0)	(0)	$ 65,885
27	42	(0)	(0)	$ 71,371
28	43	(0)	(0)	$ 77,315
29	44	(0)	(0)	$ 83,754
30	45	(0)	(0)	$ 90,728
31	46	(0)	(0)	$ 98,284
32	47	(0)	(0)	$106,469
33	48	(0)	(0)	$115,335
34	49	(0)	(0)	$124,940
35	50	(0)	(0)	$135,345
36	51	(0)	(0)	$146,616
37	52	(0)	(0)	$158,826
38	53	(0)	(0)	$172,052
39	54	(0)	(0)	$186,380
40	55	(0)	(0)	$201,902
41	56	(0)	(0)	$218,716
42	57	(0)	(0)	$236,930
43	58	(0)	(0)	$256,661
44	59	(0)	(0)	$278,035
45	60	(0)	(0)	$301,189
46	61	(0)	(0)	$326,271
47	62	(0)	(0)	**$353,442**

Total invested	$ 12,000
Total invested with the interest earned up until year 11	$ 18,321
Total interest earned @ 8% annual rate of return	$335,121
Total savings balance in the account	**$353,442**

In this scenario, Investor #5 began investing at the age of 16. The investor deposited $100 each month into his/her account on a consistent basis for 10 years. After the final deposit into the account at the end of year 10 the investor stopped saving. The investor let the money remain in the account for the next 37 years, depositing no further monies. Utilizing the average rate of return of 8%, the total account balance at the end of the 47 years would be approximately $353,442.

Investor #5 began to invest and establish his/her accounts at the age of 16, or seven years earlier than Investor #1. It may not seem like all that big of a deal, "So what, what is seven years really going to do?" Well, when you look at it in dollars and cents (or sense) it becomes instantly clear that it is a HUGE deal. Just think, by taking advantage of this program and practicing it in your life, this could be you. Both Investor #1 and Investor #5 had the *exact* same money invested, $12,000 in deposits and $18,321 including interest after 10 years. But this is, as they say, "Where the rubber meets the road." As a result, Investor #5, taking advantage of the extra seven years that the money was invested with compounding interest earned an additional – you ready for this – $151,540. Did you hear that, $151,540? WOW! How would you like to be rewarded in your life with the opportunity to increase your financial portfolio by over $150,000 by just taking the initiative and responsibility to start saving at age 16. Look at the difference that one decision can make in the future of your life.

In this scenario, Investor #6 came across this fantastic, money management program called, YOUR MONEY, DAY ONE. He decided to implement the advice and guidance that was discussed in the program and began investing at the age of 16.

Investor #6 Begins at age 16

Year	Age	Per Month	Per Year	Ending Balance Including Interest
1	16	100	$1,200	$ 1,245
2	17	100	$1,200	$ 2,594
3	18	100	$1,200	$ 4,055
4	19	100	$1,200	$ 5,638
5	20	100	$1,200	$ 7,353
6	21	100	$1,200	$ 9,210
7	22	100	$1,200	$ 11,222
8	23	100	$1,200	$ 13,402
9	24	100	$1,200	$ 15,763
10	25	100	$1,200	$ 18,321
11	26	100	$1,200	$ 21,092
12	27	100	$1,200	$ 24,094
13	28	100	$1,200	$ 27,345

Investor #6, cont.

14	29	100	$1,200	$ 30,867
15	30	100	$1,200	$ 34,683
16	31	100	$1,200	$ 38,817
17	32	100	$1,200	$ 43,294
18	33	100	$1,200	$ 48,145
19	34	100	$1,200	$ 53,399
20	35	100	$1,200	$ 59,091
21	36	100	$1,200	$ 65,258
22	37	100	$1,200	$ 71,937
23	38	100	$1,200	$ 79,173
24	39	100	$1,200	$ 87,012
25	40	100	$1,200	$ 95,503
26	41	100	$1,200	$104,701
27	42	100	$1,200	$114,666
28	43	100	$1,200	$125,460
29	44	100	$1,200	$137,153
30	45	100	$1,200	$149,820
31	46	100	$1,200	$163,541
32	47	100	$1,200	$178,406
33	48	100	$1,200	$194,508
34	49	100	$1,200	$211,952
35	50	100	$1,200	$230,848
36	51	100	$1,200	$251,317
37	52	100	$1,200	$273,491
38	53	100	$1,200	$297,512
39	54	100	$1,200	$323,533
40	55	100	$1,200	$351,722
41	56	100	$1,200	$382,257
42	57	100	$1,200	$415,336
43	58	100	$1,200	$451,169
44	59	100	$1,200	$489,986
45	60	100	$1,200	$532,036
46	61	100	$1,200	$577,588
47	62	100	$1,200	**$626,933**

Total invested	$ 56,400
Total interest earned @ 8% annual rate of return	$570,533
Total savings balance in the account	**$626,933**

Investor #6, a very intelligent kid, named Michael, deposited $100 each month into his account on a consistent basis and continued to do so for 47 years, until the age of 62. Utilizing the average rate of return of 8%, the total account balance at the end of the 47 years would be approximately $626,933. Just think, from taking the time to read this book, which at the time seemed to be a little lame, Investor #6 was able to acquire over a half-a-million dollars. HALF-A-MILLION DOLLARS. WOW!!!! Who would have ever thought that would be possible?

Investor Scenario Comparison Chart 2

Total Money Invested	Length of Investment	Length of Growth (years)	Ending Balance
Investor #1			
$12,000	10	40	$201,902
Investor #5			
$12,000	10	47	$353,442
Investor #6			
$56,400	47	47	$626,933

Take some time to review and analyze the scenario involving Investor #6. This is the bread and butter of this program; begin early, establish a mutual fund, be persistent, be diligent, persevere and let that precious commodity – time – do its thing. Don't try to picture yourself at the age of 62, but take the necessary steps to effectively plan and prepare yourself for when that time comes, because it will. You can see the difference, 'the proof is in the pudding.'

For the ease of comparing scenarios, we have shown that Investor #6 deposits a mere $100 a month, but if you follow the budgeting program and invest 10% of your net pay, over your career, you will be setting aside *far more than $100 per month* into your account. Again, by taking advantage of time, compounding interest and good savings habits, your retirement accounts will have a far greater chance of reaching seven figures, that's over $1 million!

Investor Scenario Comparison Summary Chart

	Total Money Invested	Length of Investment	Length of Growth (years)	Ending Balance
Investor #1	$12,000	10	40	$201,902
Investor #2	$36,000	30	30	$149,820
Investor #3	$48,000	40	40	$351,722
Investor #4	$24,000	20	20	$ 59,091
Investor #4-W	$142,853	20	20	$351,724
Investor #5	$12,000	10	47	$353,442
Investor #6	$56,400	47	47	$626,933

There is a lot of information and data covered in these tables. As you review the concept of compound interest using the various scenarios as examples, you will gain a thorough understanding of just how important an impact it can have on your financial future. Spend a little extra time reviewing the examples and see how much difference there is between them. Think about which investor you want to be. This is a clear example of how time and compound interest can make all the difference. Ask yourself, **"Will you control your money or will your money control you?"**

The following Compound Interest Comparison Table shows in detail some very valuable and important information. It indicates the specific differential among the total dollars invested, the number of years the money is invested and the various rates of return possible. Please review the information contained in the table. You will gain a clear understanding of how important the role of time and compound interest is on saving money.

Compound Interest Comparison Table

The result of putting off investing and the result of lost time.
Scenario: Investing $100 per month, invested for the number of years indicated in the Years Invested column.
The retirement age of 62 has been used for this example.

Age	Total $$ Invested	Yrs. Invested	6%	7%	Rate of Return 8%	9%	10%
16	$56,400	47	$314,697	$441,626	$626,933	$899,145	$1,302,250
	Differential		($19,487)	($31,009)	($49,345)	($78,522)	($125,951)
17	$55,200	46	$295,210	$410,617	$577,588	$820,623	$1,176,299
	Differential		($18,352)	($28,914)	($45,552)	($71,765)	($113,062)
18	$54,000	45	$276,858	$381,703	$532,036	$748,858	$1,063,237
	Differential		($17,284)	($26,958)	($42,050)	($65,589)	($102,304)
19	$52,800	44	$259,574	$354,745	$489,986	$683,269	960,933
	Differential		($16,277)	($25,137)	($38,817)	($59,944)	($ 92,570)
20	$51,600	43	$243,297	$329,608	$451,169	$623,325	868,363
	Differential		($15,329)	($23,437)	($35,833)	($54,787)	($ 83,762)
21	$50,400	42	$227,968	$306,171	$415,336	$568,538	784,601
	Differential		($14,437)	($21,852)	($33,079)	($50,070)	($ 75,792)
22	$49,200	41	$213,531	$284,319	$382,257	$518,468	708,809
	Differential		($13,595)	($20,376)	($30,536)	($45,762)	($ 68,580)
23	$48,000	40	$199,936	$263,943	$351,721	$472,706	640,229

Meaning of differential: This number represents the difference in the amount of money, from one year to the next, by waiting to invest just $1,200.00 and by waiting just an additional 12 months.

Source: http://www.banksite.com/calc/savings

The Golden Years

You should take advantage of your young age and **begin saving for your future NOW** while you have time on your side. Putting it off, as you can see, can significantly impact your life. Developing sound personal money management skills is one of the most important life skills you will need. We have discussed in detail how critical it is to properly plan for your financial well being when you reach those *golden years*. To successfully plan for those years it will be crucial for you to have developed a financial program that will enable you to live the life that you want, need and deserve. We have discussed building that investment portfolio, or '**nest egg**' as it is often referred, the money that you will need to live on when you are no longer working. However, if you do not effectively plan for this time in your life, you may end up having to continue to work well past the age that you may desire. In a 2001 survey of baby boomers (someone born between 1946-1964), **80% said they were planning to work past 65, at least part time**, according to AARP (American Association of Retired Persons). Many will do it because they have to; they need the money, AARP says. This generation has every expectation that they will live longer than the previous one. Yet, few have saved enough money for 30 years of full retirement.[4]

In a study conducted by the AARP in March 2006, the following are the responses to the question, "What are the major reasons for working in retirement?"

> 61% Need the money
> 54% Desire to stay mentally active
> 52% Need the health benefits
> 49% Desire to stay physically active
> 47% Desire to remain productive or useful

The one response that I want you to pay particular attention to is the **61% who responded by saying they will need the money**. As

---

4 http://www.usatoday.com/money/perfi/retirement/2005-06-08-retiree-main_x.html

mentioned before, few have saved enough to be able to live and survive a long retirement (30 years) without working.

Social Security

The reason that we are briefly discussing this issue is that while these people, baby boomers, were living their lives, they were assuming that a government established retirement system would be taking care of them when they reached their retirement age. That system, better known as **Social Security**, operates with a simple concept: while you work, you pay taxes into the Social Security system (also known as FICA, which we previously discussed when we looked at an example of an earnings statement) and when you retire or become disabled, you receive monthly benefits that are based on your reported earnings.

The problem is that the amount of money that they paid into the Social Security system has been outpaced by the number of people that now draw, and will continue to draw, upon those funds. Therefore, the Social Security taxes that your generation pays are being used to fund current retirees. Meanwhile, the cost of living is increasing and the cost of products and services is rising, making it extremely hard for retirees to stretch the dollars they receive and causing them to face very difficult financial decisions. That is why **I empower you to take action immediately so you will not have to depend on a system over which you have no control, nor even any idea if it will meet your needs later in life**. You will often see the topic of Social Security in the news. Most recently, headlines have been centered around the increased chances that with the growth of the population and the increased cost of living, the Social Security system could potentially run out of money, leaving millions of retirees panicking and squandering to make ends meet. You do not want to be one of those people.

I am sharing this information with you not to try to create fear or scare you about a story you see on the evening news, but to share with you why it is so important to take the initiative and personal responsibility NOW, while you are young. Begin to effectively plan for a time in your life that is going to come. You do not want to find yourself in a position in which you will be looking at yourself in the mirror saying, "**I wish I would have**," because when you find yourself in that position, it will be too late.

Part II – The Head With the Mean Face

The second head of the two-headed monster must be managed so it does not manage you. **Remember interest can act like a two-headed monster; it can be your best friend or your worst enemy**. Interest can work remarkably in your favor and provide you incredible opportunities, but if not properly managed, it can create financial situations that can be damaging and can keep you from enjoying financial success and freedom.

So, how can compound interest that has been so clearly demonstrated to provide financial growth, turn into this behemoth creature called the–two-headed monster? Well, it is really plain and simple my friends, it is called – *debt*. Now we are going to elaborate not just on the word, but how debt gets created and specifically how having too much of it can literally damage and even destroy your life, your ambitions, your dreams, making you uncomfortable and miserable. That is why I take such an interest in providing this information to you, because I do not want you to experience that kind of life, especially when you can take control of it so it won't happen.

Credit Card Debt

To be financially successful you must eliminate those habits that will impede or get in the way of you achieving your financial goals. Revolving debt is one thing with which many adults struggle to manage.

We will not go into each and every possible scenario that can lead to acquiring debt, but we will concentrate on the most commonly used instrument and the result of that instrument that plagues a large majority of people, the credit card and credit card debt. According to CardWeb, a service that tracks credit card trends, statistics show that the **average debt**

per American household with at least one credit card was $9,659 in a survey in June 2007.[5] Just as a quick example before we get into the nitty gritty, let's say you have a credit card, with the average balance given by CardWeb of $9,659, at an interest rate of 18%. Your beginning monthly payment would be $240.03 according to the credit card company's minimum payment guidelines. Assuming that you did not charge any further purchases, the length of payments would be 384 months. Can you believe that, 384 months? Have you converted it yet from months to years? Here, let me help you in case you don't have a calculator handy. It would calculate out to 32 years! This is actually longer than taking out the standard home loan of 30 years, all for a lousy $9,659. Oh, by the way, one more little thing, here's why I say that interest can be your best friend or your worst enemy. Guess how much interest it would cost you over the life of the term? $14,315.51 in interest. Imagine that, you will pay more in interest than what you originally borrowed – for what?

Since we just discussed how compound interest works to build your financial future let's look at the exact same situation, but in reverse. What would it mean if instead of making payments on a credit card, you invested the same monthly payments, each month, into a mutual fund, earning on average 8% over the same term? Well, I hope you are sitting down because you would have saved $181,956.89. I have to ask: what would you rather do, pay a credit card company for 32 years, paying nearly $24,000 (including principal & interest) with little or nothing to show for it, or take that same amount of money and save it over the same time period ending up with close to $182,000? Plain and simple, that is what this program is all about; making the right money management decisions in your life.

The Minimum Payment Trap

Knowing how interest works, it is fairly clear to see what happens. Once you establish a balance on your credit card, interest begins to accrue, similar to when we looked at a savings account, but this time not in your favor. As interest is calculated, the majority of your *minimum payment*

5 http://moneycentral.msn.com/content/Banking/creditcardsmarts/P74808.asp

is made up of interest with only a small portion applied to the principal balance (the money you originally spent) outstanding. Once the payment is applied, the process then begins all over again, repeating itself until the balance is at zero. As a result, the debt you owe on the outstanding principal balance is not decreasing significantly enough. Then the interest is again calculated on the balance and the vicious cycle goes round and round, not in your favor.

Let's discuss a possible real life situation. You decide to buy a new laptop, some software, a printer, wireless equipment and some accessories. The package comes to $2,000.00. Let's look at the financial ramifications of making the minimum payment.[6]

Credit card balance of $2,000.00

Interest rate of 18%, making the minimum payment

Payment Schedule

Mo.	Payment	Interest Paid	Principal Paid	Remaining Balance
1	$49.70	$30.00	$19.70	$1,980.30
2	$49.21	$29.70	$19.51	$1,960.79
3	$48.72	$29.41	$19.31	$1,941.48
4	$48.24	$29.12	$19.12	$1,922.36
5	$47.78	$28.84	$18.94	$1,903.42
6	$47.30	$28.55	$18.75	$1,884.67
7	$46.83	$28.27	$18.56	$1,866.11
8	$46.37	$27.99	$18.38	$1,847.73
9	$45.92	$27.72	$18.20	$1,829.53
10	$45.46	$27.44	$18.02	$1,811.51
11	$45.01	$27.17	$17.84	$1,793.67
12	$44.58	$26.91	$17.67	$1,776.00
-				
225	$ 1.36	$ 0.02	$ 1.34	$ 0.00

6 http://www.bankrate.com/brm/calc/MinPayment.asp?ccBalance=2000&ccArate=18&ratio=I%2B1 &ccMinPayment=49.70&ccPayment=50.7&paymentType=high&Submit=Calculate

It will take 225 months, by making the minimum payment to pay the account balance in full. By doing so, you will pay $2,652.09 in interest over the life of the debt to borrow $2,000.00. The total repayment, principal and interest is $4,652.09. What are the chances that you will still own any of these items in 225 months or almost 19 years? What happens if you decide to upgrade after four or five years but you are still paying on the existing computer purchase? You could place yourself in a financial quandary by still paying for the old equipment while acquiring the new equipment. This is why it is so important to **develop sound personal money management skills** to properly manage situations like this so you don't find yourself in these types of circumstances.

When you get yourself into credit card debt it is astonishing how you can end up paying more in interest than the original dollar amount borrowed, and how long it will take you to pay off the balance if you just make the minimum monthly payment. Sales people will try to entice you with statements such as, "It will only cost you $50 per month," but they won't tell you how much it will cost you in the long run. This kind of financial decision making can totally impede the progress that you are trying to make and your opportunities to save money. It goes back to the *budgeting* we discussed, setting up separate accounts into which you will deposit money monthly including, **retirement savings** (long term savings), **general savings** (short term savings in which you might save for a computer, for example), an **emergency fund** (for those unexpected expenses) and **charitable giving** (helping those in need). If you put yourself in a financial position that will not allow you to do so because of debt payments, you will not be able to achieve your financial goals. It is that simple.

Real Life Case Study

I share with you a real life story that appeared in the Los Angeles Times Business section and was reported by Ms. Liz Pulliam Weston.[7] If you are interested in reading more articles and topics published by Ms.

---

7 http://www.latimes.com/business/la-fi-montalk2dec02,0,811750.column

Pulliam Weston you may find her on the MSN website at the following address: http://articles.moneycentral.msn.com/Commentary/ByAuthor/LizPulliamWeston.aspx.

Let's approach this as a case study since this is a real life story of someone who actually got themselves into a very difficult situation involving compounding interest.

Digging Out of a Credit Card Trap

December 2, 2007

Dear Liz: Last year my credit card rates averaged 7.9%. Today they average 29.9%! Because of job downsizing, I could not make two months of payments, so my credit card companies really socked it to me. My monthly minimums jumped from $200 to $2,000.

I have given up trying to salvage my once-excellent credit rating. Now all I am hoping to do is stop the $39 late and over-limit fees that get added on as "purchases" (and that get charged the outrageous interest). I also would like to stop the incessant phone calls (12 to 15 a day).

It seems like the companies are trying to force me into bankruptcy. I don't know where to turn. I can see that a credit card settlement service company is an alternative, but how do I know whom I can trust to negotiate with the creditors and follow through with the distribution of money? Do I try to do it myself? If I do succeed in "settling" for some lower amount, don't I have to pay income taxes on the amount saved? It seems like an impossible trap.

Answer: You're in a trap, all right, but it's largely one of your own making.

Carrying balances on your credit cards is a terrible idea. It encourages you to live beyond your means and leaves you vulnerable to sudden increases in your interest rates or minimum payments.

You need to get on track. Can you cut expenses or land a second job that would enable you to pay these bills?

If not, and you can't even pay the minimums, you should

talk to two professionals: a counselor with a legitimate nonprofit credit counseling agency, preferably one affiliated with the National Foundation for Credit Counseling, and an experienced bankruptcy attorney.

Credit counselors' agreements with card companies allow them to offer repayment plans at lower interest rates. But the counselors could steer you away from bankruptcy, even if that might be the best option for you. Bankruptcy attorneys, by contrast, might be inclined to steer you to court. Consulting both will ensure you get a balanced picture of your options.

Trying to settle your debt for less than what you owe is fraught with peril: Debt settlement firms tend to charge high, often hidden fees and can offer no guarantees of success (if they do offer guarantees, that is a sign to stay clear). You're likely to do further damage to what's left of your credit scores. You may get sued. Although bankruptcy stops collection efforts, including lawsuits, there's nothing to stop your creditors from suing you in the midst of debt settlement negotiations. Then there's the tax issue. As you suggested, the "forgiven" debt may be taxed as income to you.

Debt settlement is typically a reasonable option only for folks who can't repay their debt and aren't able to erase it in Chapter 7 bankruptcy liquidation. (If your income is too high or you have assets to protect, you might not be able to file for Chapter 7.) If that describes you, then your bankruptcy attorney may be able to guide you to someone who can help settle your debts.

Case Study Summary

I have a feeling that right now you are sitting there thinking WOW. This is a real life story about someone who is experiencing an uncompromising position that will affect one's financial situation and one's life for a very long time.

Let's review our 'case study.' In the opening paragraph, did you notice that the average interest rate on the credit cards went from 7.9% to 29.9%?

Do the math, the rate increased three times over. You may be saying, "Hey they can't do that; that's not right; that's not fair, the person said they were unemployed as a result of downsizing," (downsizing is when a company decides they have more employees than needed or they need to cut back as a result of economic conditions and they let employees go.) Here's a perfect example of someone who could have benefited from an emergency fund. It's real; a credit card company can actually and legally raise the credit card interest rate. Remember those papers you are supposed to take the time to read when you open a bank account, mutual fund account, or credit card account? Within the credit card disclosure information or the Cardmember Agreement, you will be informed about the possibility of an interest rate change. This action is taken when the account is considered to be in default. The account can be considered in default when you fail to make at least the minimum payment to your account by the payment date or if the method of payment, check, debit card, etc. is not honored. Missed or late payments can effect the *annual percentage rate* (APR), the rate calculated on the entire account balance, and move it into a *variable default rate*, which is a much higher percentage rate.

There is also another term called *universal default rate*. This means that when you are late paying one lender, other credit cards with which you have balances can increase the rates on those cards as well. This type of default information will be disclosed within the card agreement disclosure form. Remember, we have discussed the importance of reading *all the disclosure* forms so you will gain a thorough and complete understanding of the exact terms and conditions. The default rate can be lowered to the applicable rate again, however, you will have to make at least the minimum payment, for a set number of consecutive months, on time, before this can take place. This is an action you will want to discuss personally with a customer service representative from the credit card company.

You can see what the financial circumstances of the increase rate did to the person in this case study; suddenly they were asked to pay ten times as much PER MONTH. The payments went from $200 per month to $2,000 per month.

Bankruptcy

You can feel the desperation of the person in the case study and then when you reach the word – bankruptcy – eeeeeew! That is a word that you DO NOT WANT TO BE USING if you are trying to have a successful financial future. You may be asking yourself what is bankruptcy? *Bankruptcy* is the very last resort in a financial situation, legally declaring, through a very long and expensive court process, that you do not have the ability to continue to pay your obligations, including debt. You DO NOT WANT TO FIND YOURSELF IN THIS FINANCIAL POSITION in your life. The laws are constantly changing, making it harder and harder to declare bankruptcy and to eliminate all of your debt to try to gain a fresh start. This is no easy out; it will be extremely hard for you to obtain any future credit, including an auto loan or home mortgage for a very long time and it can also make it difficult to rent an apartment or even get a job.

As you can see, making uncalculated financial decisions can significantly impact your ability to successfully plan for your future. This is a very sad state of affairs for this person; remember *this is a real life situation*. It could be you.

Credit Rating

One of the keys to financial success is establishing and maintaining excellent credit. Credit is monitored by credit reporting agencies that maintain credit reports and assign a credit rating. A *credit report* is a file that is kept by companies that obtain and track your payment history. A *credit rating,* also known as a FICO (Fair Isaac Credit Organization) score, is the number associated with a person's payment history to assess credit worthiness. The range is between 300-850; the higher the score the better the credit rating. There will be entities that will use this score to evaluate applicants including lenders, landlords, insurance companies and employers to name a few. An excellent credit rating is very important in your life. To maintain an excellent credit rating with the credit reporting agencies; Experian, Equifax and Transunion, practice one simple rule: ALWAYS pay your bills on time. It is really that simple, practice it and you will significantly decrease the chances of placing yourself in a potentially damaging financial situation. Further, late payments result in late FEES (remember that word?), adding to an already problematic situation. Continue to ignore it and the 'incessant' phone calls from collection departments demanding payment will begin; all the while your credit rating is being negatively affected.

You are eligible, by law, to acquire a copy of your credit report, free, from each agency, once a year. If you look on the internet there are many free credit report services that will assist you in obtaining one. However, only one website is authorized by the Federal Trade Commission (FTC) to supply free annual credit reports under law:

> **www.annualcreditreport.com**

Identity Theft

Another aspect of protecting your credit rating is to insure that you do not fall prey to one of the fastest growing consumer problems, identity theft. Identity theft is when someone illegally acquires your personal information-your name, date of birth, social security number, address, etc. and literally takes over who you are from an information standpoint. According to the United States Federal Trade Commission (the official government agency that deals with this issue) identity theft is the number one type of fraud complaint received, making up 32% of the total complaints filed.[8]

Criminals obtain financial accounts in your name and go on a spending spree, sticking you with the debt and the incredible headache of proving fraud. This can have catastrophic repercussions on your credit rating and financial status and cause total upheaval in your life. To give you an idea of just how big this problem is, in 2006 over 250,000 people filed a complaint with the United States Federal Trade Commission reporting identity theft. Young adults, 18-29, totaled 29% of those filing. These statistics reflect only those who took the time to file, there are surely more

8 http://www.consumer.gov/sentinel/pubs/Top10Fraud2006.pdf

who have been affected but did not file a report.[9]

It is common place these days that we find ourselves in conversation providing personal information over mobile devices, such as a cell phone or laptop. On a recent vacation, my wife and I were at Los Angeles International Airport awaiting our departure. As my wife sat there she overheard a man, nearby, on his cell phone. She deciphered that he was booking some sort of travel arrangements and suddenly he gave his credit card number and expiration date over the phone, all within ear shot of dozens of people. Anyone could have been sitting there writing all of his information down without him noticing; he was oblivious to the danger.

Unfortunately, we live in a world in which there are many dishonest people lurking about that make a living taking advantage of others. This is a growing problem that affects millions of people. That is why it is important to maintain a close guard on your personal information at all times. Check all of your accounts and report suspicious activity immediately. Get in the habit of pulling a credit report annually to monitor any activity reported that is not yours. You work hard to build your positive credit rating, take the extra step and maintain it by paying attention to your accounts and safe guarding your personal information. In the hands of the wrong person it can cause serious problems for you.

That little two by three piece of plastic that fits in your wallet has the enormous capability to affect so many areas of your life. We have discussed many in detail. **It takes patience, perseverance and discipline to fight off the temptations that will create a vacuum and suck your money right out of your pockets**. Don't get me wrong, I am just like the next guy, I want to have nice things in my life, I want to have fun, I want to enjoy myself – but in order to do so, we must understand the limits so as not to make drastic mistakes. Sure, I may be asking you to not eat out as often, not buy all the clothes that you want, not buy every electronic gizmo and to limit your downloads from iTunes, but you can enjoy these things if you develop good habits of personal money management that will allow you to live within your means. It's simple. Manage your money, make

9 http://www.consumer.gov/sentinel/pubs/Top10Fraud2006.pdf

smart purchases and do not allow yourself to become burdened with debt so that the two-headed monster stays your friend, instead of becoming your worst enemy. Ask yourself, in the end, **"Will you control your money or will your money control you?"**

This has been a very lengthy and intense section, but an important one. You have been totally awesome in applying yourself, being patient and diligent about absorbing this information. Truly, a great job. Let's move on once again.

Appendix

Equifax
P.O. Box 740256 www.equifax.com
Atlanta, GA 30374 800-685-1111

Experian
P.O. Box 2002 www.experian.com
Allen, TX 75013 888-397-3742

Transunion LLC
P.O. Box 2000 www.transunion.com
Chester, PA 19022 800-888-4213

Chapter 12

EVERYONE KNOWS UNCLE SAM:
FILING A TAX RETURN

As a young adult your parents have probably talked to you at length about a couple of acronyms (words formed from initial letters that form an abbreviation) that can inflict a feeling of nervousness, sweaty palms, shortness of breath or just plain anxiety. These acronyms, known as the SAT and ACT, are the exams that you agonize over and that are required for you to get into college. I know for me, when I completed mine I thought, "Whew...I am glad that's over with." It is a very anxiety ridden process, especially with so much riding on it, and I am sure that your parents have had or will have more than a couple conversations with you regarding their expectations. Let's take time to explore some additional acronyms.

Acronyms

When you look around there are a lot of three letter acronyms. For example – ABC, NBC, CBS – the major television networks. Then there are the business acronyms within the investment world. Some will even ange

·¹

ıbols that identify them on the New York Stock
Target or WMT – Wal Mart. And then there are
ɔse them for their company names like – GMC –
ıtion and KFC – Kentucky Fried Chicken.

y asking yourself why we are going through what
exercise in exploring what acronyms mean and what
n't using them. Well there is one acronym in particular
y the most recognized acronym among the American
ɔn. It is associated with a variety of reactions and emotions that
ɪange from respect, because the country needs it, to hatred for the service
it performs, to utter confusion because of the complexity of the system it
monitors. But the one thing that this acronym does require from you is your
attention, your respect and your ability to understand how it is going to be
a part of your life, like it or not. It will also be important for you to abide
by the rules that have been established or it can become very unpleasant
and possibly financially debilitating. The acronym that you will become
very familiar with when you start working is the IRS. This stands for the
Internal Revenue Service.

The IRS

The *IRS* is part of the United States Government Treasury Department
and is responsible for administering and enforcing its laws, policies and
procedures. It is officially the federal agency of the government that is
responsible for properly collecting *federal income taxes* in the United
States. Some of you are already way too familiar with this agency, (I
hope not in a bad way, like being audited) and for the rest of you, your
introduction will come sooner than you think. While discussing a topic
such as the importance of saving your hard earned money, you should
have at least a basic understanding of what the IRS is and what it does.

There are a significant number of people out there that if you just
mention the three letters I-R-S, you would be amazed at the reactions on
their faces, even before they open their mouths and speak their opinions.
In my lifetime, I have very seldom spoken with ANYONE who had a

Your Money, Day One

kind word to say about the federal agency and I have NEVER had anyone openly jump up and down with glee and hug me to express how much they love the IRS. This is especially true if you have ever talked to anyone who has been audited, which is when the IRS has questions regarding your tax return and they meet with you to discuss it, in detail, so they can understand it better. This means that they will go through your financial record keeping, question it and seek proof as to how you arrived at the information you submitted. An audit is usually for a tax year that is in the past, often a couple years or more, requiring you to have immaculate financial record keeping and organization.

How does the IRS come into your life? When starting a job you will go through orientation. You will be trained on the important personnel issues of the company. During this process there will be a plethora of topics and issues covering things like work schedules, required breaks, dress code, sexual harassment policy, vacation, holidays, benefits, safety, reasons for termination and a variety of other topics. One topic that will be covered in detail is establishing yourself with the IRS by completing the W-4 Form, the Employee's Withholding Allowance Certificate form.

W-4 Form

The purpose of the *W-4 Form - Employee's Withholding Allowance Certificate* is to allow the employer to withhold the correct Federal and State income tax from your wages. By completing this form (W-4) you will be estimating your tax liability and will have it withheld from your earnings. Other mandatory withholdings such as Social Security (FICA) and Medicare, are predetermined. At the end of the year when you file a tax return it will be determined if the amount of money withheld was equal to the amount actually due, as calculated by the IRS. That is when it is determined if you are entitled to a refund or if you owe money. This is really the whole idea of filing a tax return.

It should be known that the W-4 form is not optional when you begin work, but a REQUIREMENT, for you to fill out completely, signing and dating it. It is extremely important that you make sure that your social

-136-

security number is correct and printed legibly since this number is going to be associated with everything you do when it comes to your government financial records. Become familiar with the form. Read it in its entirety and gain a basic understanding of it. If you have questions, you can ask your parents, a tax professional, your human resource director or you can call the IRS (800-829-1040) and they will be happy to answer any questions you may have. You may also access the website at www.irs.gov.

Get used to requirements from the IRS because there will be many, including the requirement for you to properly file a tax return. A tax return utilizes forms established by the Internal Revenue Service that require individuals and businesses to report to the United States government the proper calculation of income tax to be paid based upon earnings from employment or business operations. Form a habit of filing a tax return within the specified tax laws established by the United States government, specifically the IRS and the U.S. Treasury Department, as failure to do so will bring you a boatload of problems and could even land you in jail.

W-2 Form

After the end of a calendar year you will receive another form, called a *W-2 Form - Wage and Tax Statement*. The W-2 is the summary of the taxes and certain deductions that have been withheld from your wages for the year. A W-2 is legally required to be prepared for you by your employer and must be provided to you by January 31st of the calendar year following the previous tax year. The form comes with various copies that are to be used when you file your taxes. The W-2 will have the following information contained in it that will be used.[1] All the information contained on the W-2 will be in specific boxes, identified by lower case alphabetical letters or numbers (See form on page 140).

a- Employees Social Security Number
b- Employer identification number (EIN)
c- Employer's name, address, and ZIP code

---

1 http://www.taxesindepth.com/info-w2-form.html

d- Control Number

e- Employee's first name and initial, last name, suffix

f- Employer's address and ZIP code

1- Wages, tips, other compensation (the total of your taxable wages, tips, other compensation and taxable fringe benefits)

2- Federal income tax withheld (the total amount of federal income tax that was withheld from your salary)

3- Social security wages (the total in wages that were subject to the social security tax)

4- Social security tax withheld (the total amount of social security tax withheld from your salary)

5- Medicare wages and tips (the total of your wages and tips that are subject to Medicare tax)

6- Medicare tax withheld (the total you paid in Medicare tax already.)

7- Social security tips

8- Allocated tips (the total in allocated tips)

9- Advance EIC payment (your Advance Earned Income payment)

10- Dependent care benefits (the total in dependent care benefits)

11- Nonqualified plans (a distribution made to you from a non-qualified deferred compensation plan or nongovernmental section 457 plan)

12a- See instructions for box 12

13- Statutory employee, Retirement plan, Third party sick pay (may have a box checked that indicates whether you are a statutory employee, a participant of your employer's retirement plan or received third party sick pay)

14- Other (records any other information for the employee, such as union dues, health insurance premiums, and educational assistance payments)

15- State Employer's state ID number

16- State wages, tips, etc. (your state wages, tips and compensation)

17- State income tax (total state income tax you paid)

18- Local wages, tips, etc. (your local wages, tips and compensation)

19- Local income tax

20- Locality name

There is an abundance of information that is provided on a W-2 form. Don't get overwhelmed by it. When it comes down to actually filing a basic *tax return*, like the form 1040-EZ, you will only be utilizing a limited amount of the information. There are also blank boxes with no information at all. The more you work, the more information you will notice appearing on the form. Look it over to become familiar with it and realize what it contains.

As with the W-4, read it, understand it and ask appropriate questions. Each copy of the W-2 form is identified with a specific purpose. For instance:

- Copy 1 – For State, City or Local Tax Department
- Copy B – To Be Filed With Employee's FEDERAL Tax Return
- Copy C – For EMPLOYEE'S RECORDS
- Copy 2 – To Be Filed With Employee's State, City or Local Income Tax Return
- Copy D – For Employer

In the left hand corner of the form you should pay particularly close attention to, "This information is being furnished to the Internal Revenue Service." **Understand that the information that you have been given has also been supplied to the IRS**. This is why it is important to report the information on your tax return properly because the IRS is obtaining the information as well. You must review all the information to insure its accuracy immediately upon receiving your W-2. It is especially important to insure that the social security number within box 'a' is yours and it is correct. If it is not, you should IMMEDIATELY contact your supervisor or human resource director to correct the error.

22222

a Employee's social security number

OMB No. 1545-0008

b Employer identification number (EIN)

c Employer's name, address, and ZIP code

d Control number

e Employee's first name and initial   Last name   Suff.

f Employee's address and ZIP code

1 Wages, tips, other compensation
2 Federal income tax withheld
3 Social security wages
4 Social security tax withheld
5 Medicare wages and tips
6 Medicare tax withheld
7 Social security tips
8 Allocated tips
9 Advance EIC payment
10 Dependent care benefits
11 Nonqualified plans
12a Code
13 Statutory employee / Retirement plan / Third-party sick pay
12b Code
14 Other
12c Code
12d Code

15 State   Employer's state ID number
16 State wages, tips, etc.
17 State income tax
18 Local wages, tips, etc.
19 Local income tax
20 Locality name

Form **W-2** **Wage and Tax Statement**

2009

Department of the Treasury—Internal Revenue Service

Copy 1—For State, City, or Local Tax Department

Department of the Treasury—Internal Revenue Service

Form 1040EZ

Income Tax Return for Single and Joint Filers With No Dependents (99) **2008**

OMB No. 1545-0074

Label (See page 9.) Use the IRS label. Otherwise, please print or type.

Your first name and initial | Last name | Your social security number

If a joint return, spouse's first name and initial | Last name | Spouse's social security number

Home address (number and street). If you have a P.O. box, see page 9. | Apt. no.

City, town or post office, state, and ZIP code. If you have a foreign address, see page 9.

▲ You **must** enter your SSN(s) above. ▲

Presidential Election Campaign (page 9)

Checking a box below will not change your tax or refund.

Check here if you, or your spouse if a joint return, want $3 to go to this fund . . . ▶ ☐ You ☐ Spouse

Income

Attach Form(s) W-2 here.

Enclose, but do not attach, any payment.

1 Wages, salaries, and tips. This should be shown in box 1 of your Form(s) W-2. Attach your Form(s) W-2. | 1

2 Taxable interest. If the total is over $1,500, you cannot use Form 1040EZ. | 2

3 Unemployment compensation and Alaska Permanent Fund dividends (see page 11). | 3

4 Add lines 1, 2, and 3. This is your **adjusted gross income.** | 4

5 If someone can claim you (or your spouse if a joint return) as a dependent, check the applicable box(es) below and enter the amount from the worksheet on back.
☐ You ☐ Spouse
If no one can claim you (or your spouse if a joint return), enter $8,950 if **single;** $17,900 if **married filing jointly.** See back for explanation. | 5

6 Subtract line 5 from line 4. If line 5 is larger than line 4, enter -0-. This is your **taxable income.** ▶ | 6

Payments and tax

7 Federal income tax withheld from box 2 of your Form(s) W-2. | 7

8a **Earned income credit (EIC)** (see page 12). | 8a

b Nontaxable combat pay election. | 8b

9 Recovery rebate credit (see worksheet on pages 17 and 18). | 9

10 Add lines 7, 8a, and 9. These are your **total payments.** ▶ | 10

11 **Tax.** Use the amount on **line 6 above** to find your tax in the tax table on pages 28–36 of the booklet. Then, enter the tax from the table on this line. | 11

Refund

Have it directly deposited! See page 18 and fill in 12b, 12c, and 12d or Form 8888.

12a If line 10 is larger than line 11, subtract line 11 from line 10. This is your **refund.** If Form 8888 is attached, check here ▶ ☐ | 12a

▶ b Routing number | ▶ c Type: ☐ Checking ☐ Savings

▶ d Account number

Amount you owe

13 If line 11 is larger than line 10, subtract line 10 from line 11. This is the **amount you owe.** For details on how to pay, see page 19. ▶ | 13

Third party designee

Do you want to allow another person to discuss this return with the IRS (see page 20)? ☐ **Yes.** Complete the following. ☐ **No**

Designee's name ▶ | Phone no. ▶ ( ) | Personal identification number (PIN) ▶

Sign here

Joint return? See page 6.

Keep a copy for your records.

Under penalties of perjury, I declare that I have examined this return, and to the best of my knowledge and belief, it is true, correct, and accurately lists all amounts and sources of income I received during the tax year. Declaration of preparer (other than the taxpayer) is based on all information of which the preparer has any knowledge.

Your signature | Date | Your occupation | Daytime phone number ( )

Spouse's signature. If a joint return, **both** must sign. | Date | Spouse's occupation

Paid preparer's use only

Preparer's signature | Date | Check if self-employed ☐ | Preparer's SSN or PTIN

Firm's name (or yours if self-employed), address, and ZIP code | EIN | Phone no. ( )

For Disclosure, Privacy Act, and Paperwork Reduction Act Notice, see page 37. | Cat. No. 11329W | Form **1040EZ** (2008)

-141-

Form 1040EZ (2008)   Page **2**

Use this form if

- Your filing status is single or married filing jointly. If you are not sure about your filing status, see page 6.
- You (and your spouse if married filing jointly) were under age 65 and not blind at the end of 2008. If you were born on January 1, 1944, you are considered to be age 65 at the end of 2008.
- You do not claim any dependents. For information on dependents, see Pub. 501.
- Your taxable income (line 6) is less than $100,000.
- You do not claim any adjustments to income. For information on adjustments to income, use TeleTax topics 451–453 and 455–458 (see page 27).
- The only tax credits you can claim are the earned income credit (EIC) and the recovery rebate credit. You do not need a qualifying child to claim the EIC. For information on credits, use TeleTax topics 601, 602, 607, 608, 610, and 611 (see page 27).
- You had only wages, salaries, tips, taxable scholarship or fellowship grants, unemployment compensation, or Alaska Permanent Fund dividends, and your taxable interest was not over $1,500. But if you earned tips, including allocated tips, that are not included in box 5 and box 7 of your Form W-2, you may not be able to use Form 1040EZ (see page 10). If you are planning to use Form 1040EZ for a child who received Alaska Permanent Fund dividends, see page 11.
- You did not receive any advance earned income credit payments. If you cannot use this form, use TeleTax topic 352 (see page 27).

Filling in your return

For tips on how to avoid common mistakes, see page 22.

If you received a scholarship or fellowship grant or tax-exempt interest income, such as on municipal bonds, see the booklet before filling in the form. Also, see the booklet if you received a Form 1099-INT showing federal income tax withheld or if federal income tax was withheld from your unemployment compensation or Alaska Permanent Fund dividends.

Remember, you must report all wages, salaries, and tips even if you do not get a Form W-2 from your employer. You must also report all your taxable interest, including interest from banks, savings and loans, credit unions, etc., even if you do not get a Form 1099-INT.

Worksheet for dependents who checked one or both boxes on line 5

(keep a copy for your records)

Use this worksheet to figure the amount to enter on line 5 if someone can claim you (or your spouse if married filing jointly) as a dependent, even if that person chooses not to do so. To find out if someone can claim you as a dependent, see Pub. 501.

A. Amount, if any, from line 1 on front . _____

                             +   300.00   Enter total ▶   **A.** _____

B. Minimum standard deduction . . . . **B.** _____900.00____

C. Enter the **larger** of line A or line B here . . . . **C.** _____

D. Maximum standard deduction. If **single**, enter $5,450; if **married filing jointly**, enter $10,900 . . . . **D.** _____

E. Enter the **smaller** of line C or line D here. This is your standard deduction   **E.** _____

F. Exemption amount.
    ● If single, enter -0-.
    ● If married filing jointly and—   **F.** _____
      —both you and your spouse can be claimed as dependents, enter -0-.
      —only one of you can be claimed as a dependent, enter $3,500.

G. Add lines E and F. Enter the total here and on line 5 on the front . . .   **G.** _____

If you did not check any boxes on line 5, enter on line 5 the amount shown below that applies to you.

- Single, enter $8,950. This is the total of your standard deduction ($5,450) and your exemption ($3,500).
- Married filing jointly, enter $17,900. This is the total of your standard deduction ($10,900), your exemption ($3,500), and your spouse's exemption ($3,500).

Mailing return

Mail your return by **April 15, 2009.** Use the envelope that came with your booklet. If you do not have that envelope or if you moved during the year, see the back cover for the address to use.

Form **1040EZ** (2008)

 Printed on recycled paper

Form 1040EZ

We will be discussing the form that you as a young adult will most likely be using when filing a tax return, the *Form 1040EZ*. This form is appropriately titled – Income Tax Return for Single and Joint Filers With No Dependents. When completing a tax return you will have some options. First and foremost, you can ask your parents if they have a tax accountant or advisor. This is a great way to establish a relationship with a professional who already knows your parents and would be happy to have you as a referral. Once you begin using someone, develop a relationship with them. Get to know them and become comfortable with them as the business relationship could last a very long time. Another way for you to file taxes is by doing it yourself, handwriting the information in the appropriate corresponding boxes on the tax return form. If you choose to do so, make sure that your handwriting is very clear and legible. You also have the choice to go to the IRS website, www.irs.gov and complete the form on their website. It will be neat and typewritten. There is also the option for you to utilize a tax preparation service such as H&R Block or Jackson Hewitt, tax preparation franchises that are independently owned and operated and have trained professionals to assist you in preparing your tax return. Some companies, such as H&R Block, allow you to file your tax return online by utilizing their website, www.hrblock.com. If you choose to use this type of a tax preparation service, they will charge you a fee (there is that word again) for completing the return. Finally you can file your tax return by purchasing and using one of the various computerized software tax preparation programs such as Turbo Tax from Quicken, H&R Block's Tax Cut or Tax Act. These tax preparation programs take some time to set up but once established will guide you through the necessary steps to complete your tax return in its entirety.

Important: Proofreading is critical in filing a tax return; make sure the addition and subtraction are correct. Accuracy is key!

Filing a Tax Return

When it comes to figuring out the information concerning your taxes, much of it can be very complicated and confusing. That is why I mention that this is one of those times that having the expertise of a tax professional can be money well spent. However, there are some basic guidelines that can help. Let's look at the actual IRS requirements for filing a tax return.

The following kinds of income, often received by students, are generally taxable.[2]

- Pay for services performed

- Self-employment income

- Investment income

- Certain scholarships and fellowships

The major item that we will discuss is pay for services performed. This will generally be the wages, including tips, which you will receive from your employer for work. As stated before, your wages and tax information will be maintained by your employer. Your information will be summarized on every earnings statement you receive and then the official year-to-date summary will be disclosed when you receive your W-2 at year's end. Here are the guidelines that will help you determine if you need to file a tax return.

Claimed by a Guardian

If your parent or guardian is claiming you as a dependent on their tax return (which normally will happen if you are living with them and you are under the age of 18), you must file a return if any of the following apply:

1. Your unearned income (Interest & Dividends) was more than $850
2. Your earned income (Wages) was more than $5,350

2 http://www.irs.gov/individuals/students/article/0,,id=96674,00.html

3. Your gross income (total of your earned and unearned income) was greater than the larger of:
    a. $850, or
    b. Your earned income (up to $5,050) plus $300

To clarify this point let's look at a couple of examples.

Example #1

You have unearned income of $100 and earned income of $200. Your gross income is $300. Now you ask the question which is greater? a. $850 or b. your earned income ($200) plus $300 (which equals $500 in this scenario.) In this case a. is greater than b. and your gross income is less than a. so you do not need to file a tax return.

Example #2

You have unearned income of $500 and earned income of $5000. Your gross income is $5,500. Now you ask the question which is greater? a. $850 or b. your earned income ($5000) plus $300 (which equals $5300 in this scenario.) In this case b. is greater than a. and your gross income is more than b. so you need to file a tax return.

Not Claimed by a Guardian

If your parent (or someone else) *is not* claiming you as a dependent on their tax return then the following information can be used to determine if you are required to file a tax return:

You are single and under the age of 65 years old and your gross income was at least $ 8,750

In addition to these two scenarios, the IRS addresses filing requirements for most taxpayers to assist them in determining if they need to file a tax return. To obtain assistance use the IRS website, www.irs.gov.

The IRS provides a comprehensive guide entitled Publication 17 that will explain in detail the multiple filing scenarios.

Tips & Cash

When it comes to collecting tips or cash for services you provide, it can sometimes be a sticky and troublesome situation. Understanding it can help alleviate any future problems. If you are working at a business, such as a restaurant, coffee shop or hotel or for service providers such as salon services, delivery services or any service positions in which you may receive cash tips for performing a certain service, this money is considered income and will need to be reported. **As stated by the IRS, all tips you receive are income, and subject to income tax**. This includes tips customers give you directly, tips customers charge on credit cards and your share of tips split with other employees.[3]

Keep a daily record or other proof of your tips. (You can use IRS Form 4070A, Employee's Daily Record of Tips.) Your daily record must show your name and address, your employer's name, and the establishment's name. For each day worked, you must show the amount of cash and charged tips you received from customers or other employees, a list of the names and amounts you paid to other employees through tip splitting, and the value of any non-cash tips you get, such as tickets, passes, or other items of value. Record this information on or near the date you receive the tip income.

You are responsible for reporting tips to your employer. If you receive cash, check, or credit card tips of $20 or more in any one calendar month while working for one employer, you must report the total amount of your tips to your employer by the 10th day of the next month. If you are working at a job where receiving tips is common, make sure you discuss this with your supervisor or manager so you can gain a complete understanding of correct policies and procedures. You are responsible for understanding the information – it is your job.

---

3 http://www.irs.gov/govt/tribes/article/0,,id=140005,00.html

Investment Income

Since you are going to establish a financial portfolio using various products and services, there will be tax ramifications and implications that you will need to address. All interest gained on savings accounts, mutual funds and the like is considered unearned income and is taxable unless it is invested in an IRA. Again, this is another one of those life moments in which consulting a tax professional can be invaluable.

Scholarships & Fellowships

You also need to pay particular attention to any scholarships and fellowships that you may receive when you go to college. This money may need to be included in your tax return filing. (Again if you have any questions regarding this type of information please seek some professional advice.) If you received a scholarship or fellowship, all or part of it may be taxable, even if you did not receive a W-2 Form. Generally, the entire amount is taxable if you are not a candidate for a degree. If you are a candidate for a degree, all or part of the amount you receive may be tax free if the grant is used for tuition and fees required for enrollment and attendance, fees, books, supplies, or equipment required for your courses.[4] For further information please visit the IRS website, www.irs.gov – publication 970, Tax Benefits for Education.

Refund Money

As complex and complicated as this whole tax business can be, it also may provide you an opportunity to get back some money that is rightfully yours. If you have worked and you had federal taxes withheld from your wages, but you haven't met the defined requirements for filing a tax return you will still need to file a tax return. Why you ask? Because the IRS (as indicated on its website and in its printed periodicals) will advise you of the following:[5]

---

4 http://www.irs.gov/businesses/small/international/article/0,,id=106193,00.html
5 http://www.irs.gov/pub/irs-pdf/i1040ez.pdf (page 5)

> **Even if you do not have to file, you should file a federal income tax return to get money back if you had federal income tax withheld from your pay.**

As much as the IRS gets a bad rap for the service it performs it also makes sure that people understand that a refund may be available by filing the proper tax return. If you only remember one key point from this chapter please remember that. Why give *your* money to someone else when you have worked hard to earn it, especially when they are advising you to reclaim it? Remember that we talked earlier about ways of obtaining money. This is one of those ways. You have lived without this money so continue to develop sound savings habits and set all the money aside.

Filing Deadline

There has been a lot of emphasis on the filing of a tax return. However, there is one last thing that you will need to know. The **official tax filing deadline**, the date by which you must electronically submit it or mail it to the IRS is **April 15**. If the 15th falls on a Saturday or Sunday, then it may be due on the following Monday. The IRS website, www.irs.gov posts the official date every year.

State Income Tax

Along with having Federal Income Tax withheld from your wages, you may also have *State Income Tax* withheld, with the exception of seven states that have no state income tax: Alaska, Florida, Nevada, South Dakota, Texas, Washington and Wyoming. Two others, New Hampshire and Tennessee, tax only dividend and interest income. As with the IRS and Federal Income Tax, the forms are universal and are used by everyone filing a federal tax return. For each individual state, forms will vary. If you had state income tax withheld from your wages you will also have to file a state tax return with the corresponding tax authority in your state. You will find in the appendix section a complete listing of all the states and their corresponding websites to assist you in obtaining information regarding filing state tax returns.

Tax Code

As mentioned before, there are tax professionals that provide tax services to the general public. These professionals have countless hours of practical experience, years of education, and have completed rigorous testing along with continuing education courses to be able to perform this very important function. To give you a clear idea of how in-depth the tax laws are for us as citizens of the United States, according to the United States Government Printing Office (www.gpo.gov), Title 26 of the U.S. Code of Federal Regulations (which is the part written by the IRS) consists of 20 volumes and is 13,458 pages long. If that isn't enough for you, you can obtain the full text version of Title 26 of the United States Code which will add an additional 3,387 pages for a grand total of 16,845 pages. (This was as of 2006). Obviously there is no way and no need to cover it all. This information is the bare minimum and will give you a very basic understanding of what is involved in filing a tax return. It will be your responsibility to take some initiative and research, learn and understand above and beyond what is shared here and, when necessary, consult a professional.

Character & Integrity

As we come to the end of this chapter let's talk about an issue that surrounds the entire process of filing your taxes and how it can be a true reflection of the kind and type of person you are. Let's discuss for a moment, character building. You might ask, "How does filing your taxes have anything to do with character building or the type of person you are?" Well, it does because when it comes to filing your taxes you are talking about money, moolah, cold hard cash, either when you receive a refund, which is when you get money back from the IRS or when you owe money to the IRS. Oh, yeah, we haven't even talked about that. Yes, you can owe money to the IRS. This is when you do not have enough money withheld from your wages over the year to match what the IRS says you owe, based upon your total wages. This may become more of an issue as you progress in your life and you begin to exceed certain levels of income. But let's get back to how character building relates to filing tax returns. There is a general belief that people cheat when it comes to filing their tax returns. What do I mean by cheat? Well, let's just say that people who do cheat on their taxes aren't being 'completely honest' in reporting all of the required and necessary information on their tax return. You may ask, "But isn't the IRS getting your income information sent directly to them?" Yes, but it is the other information that they are relying upon you to disclose on your tax return with which people may take advantage of the system.

No Cheating

How many people cheat? Nobody knows exactly. But it must be a lot, because the IRS says unreported income costs the U.S. Treasury $250 billion or more a year in lost taxes.[6] According to a research study conducted by Pew Research Center in 2005, it was reported that 79% of the participants polled think it's morally wrong to not report all income for tax purposes.[7] The study doesn't conclude that the remaining 21% of the people believe it is okay, but it does beg the question, what do the other 21% believe? It is important to stand true to yourself and conduct yourself as the honest, law abiding young citizen you are. As a citizen of the United States you enjoy the opportunity to live here and be a part of one of, if not, *the* greatest countries of all. We pay taxes to create, support and maintain the country of the United States. I empower you to stay true to yourself and your country and do the right thing when it comes to following the established laws of the United States Government. If not, you are going to run the risk of experiencing, firsthand, how uncomfortable it is to go through an audit from the Internal Revenue Service (it can happen at the state level as well). Without rehashing all the details that could surround such an unpleasant experience, you should understand that this is not

6 http://www.livescience.com/strangenews/060328_pew_survey.html
7 http://www.livescience.com/mysteries/070411_tax_cheats.html

something to which you want to subject yourself. It ranks right up there with bankruptcy, which we talked about earlier. It can become a very difficult and potentially damaging financial situation that can easily be avoided. When you use a tax professional, this vulnerability can be significantly reduced because they are not willing to put their professional reputation on the line knowing they could potentially be misrepresenting financial information to the IRS, and could also be held liable for any wrong doing. By being a law abiding tax payer of the United States, you can have a positive experience instead of lot of headaches, worrying and anxiety. It's the right thing to do. Remember, you are working on developing habits that will lead to sound personal money management skills and you do not need anything like an audit from the IRS and tax penalties to detour you from your path.

We have come to the end of yet another very long and intense section of the program. There has been an abundance of important information discussed within this chapter, especially considering that you are now getting your first taste (if you haven't filed a tax return before), of dealing with the federal government and specifically the Internal Revenue Service. This is something that will become a once a year financial component of your life, so begin early in developing effective habits including organization, accurate and precise record keeping and most important – being an honest person of sound character and integrity. You have been great and I cannot thank you enough for being so diligent and focused. Great job. Let's keep on moving.

Note: (When written the IRS requirements referred to were in place, please consult the IRS website for the most recent and updated information at www.irs.gov.)

Appendix

State Tax Agencies

Alabama Department of Revenue
www.ador.state.al.us/
Alaska Department of Revenue
www.revenue.state.ak.us/
Arizona Department of Revenue
www.revenue.state.az.us/
Arkansas Department of Finance and Administration
www.state.ar.us/dfa/
California Franchise Tax Board
www.ftb.ca.gov/
California Board of Equalization
www.boe.ca.gov/
Colorado Department of Revenue
www.revenue.state.co.us/main/home.asp
Connecticut Department of Revenue Services
www.ct.gov/drs/cwp/view.asp?a=1450&q=271472
Delaware Division of Revenue
http://revenue.delaware.gov/
District of Columbia Office of the Chief Financial Officer
http://cfo.dc.gov/cfo/site/default.asp
Florida Department of Revenue
http://dor.myflorida.com/dor/
Georgia Department of Revenue
www.etax.dor.ga.gov/
Hawaii Department of Taxation
www.state.hi.us/tax/tax.html
Idaho State Tax Commission
http://tax.idaho.gov/index.html
Illinois Department of Revenue
www.revenue.state.il.us/
Indiana Department of Revenue
www.ai.org/dor/index.html
Iowa Department of Revenue and Finance
www.state.ia.us/tax/
Kansas Department of Revenue
www.ksrevenue.org/
Kentucky Revenue Cabinet
http://revenue.ky.gov/
Louisiana Department of Revenue and Taxation
www.rev.state.la.us/
Maine Revenue Services
www.maine.gov/revenue/
Maryland Comptroller of the Treasury
www.comp.state.md.us/
Massachusetts Department of Revenue
www.mass.gov/?pageID=dorhomepage&L=1&L0=Home&sid=Ador
Michigan Department of Treasury
www.michigan.gov/treasury/
Minnesota Department of Revenue
www.taxes.state.mn.us/
Mississippi State Tax Commission
www.mstc.state.ms.us/

Missouri Department of Revenue
        http://kinetic.more.net/
Montana Department of Revenue
        http://mt.gov/revenue/
Nebraska Department of Revenue
        www.revenue.state.ne.us/
Nevada Department of Taxation
        http://tax.state.nv.us/
New Hampshire Department of Revenue Administration
        www.nh.gov/revenue/
New Jersey Division of Taxation
        www.state.nj.us/treasury/taxation/
New Mexico Taxation and Revenue Department
        www.tax.state.nm.us/
New York Department of Taxation and Finance
        www.tax.state.ny.us/
North Carolina Department of Revenue
        www.dor.state.nc.us/
North Dakota State Tax Department
        www.nd.gov/tax//
Ohio Department of Taxation
        http://tax.ohio.gov/
Oklahoma Tax Commission
        www.oktax.state.ok.us/
Oregon Department of Revenue
        www.oregon.gov/DOR/
Pennsylvania Department of Revenue
        www.revenue.state.pa.us/
Rhode Island Division of Taxation
        www.tax.state.ri.us/
South Carolina Department of Revenue
        www.sctax.org/default.html
South Dakota Department of Revenue
        www.state.sd.us/drr2/revenue.html
Tennessee Department of Revenue
        www.state.tn.us/revenue/
Texas Comptroller of Public Accounts
        www.cpa.state.tx.us/
Utah State Tax Commission
        http://tax.utah.gov/
Vermont Department of Taxes
        www.state.vt.us/tax/
Virginia Department of Taxation
        www.tax.virginia.gov/
Washington Department of Revenue
        http://dor.wa.gov/content/home/
West Virginia State Tax Department
        www.state.wv.us/taxdiv/
Wisconsin Department of Revenue
        www.dor.state.wi.us/
Wyoming Department of Revenue
        http://revenue.state.wy.us/

Provided by the Tax and Accounting Sites Directory, sponsored by Accountants World. www.taxsites.com/agencies.html

Chapter 13

THE BIG 3

Y ou probably feel like all I have been doing is repeating myself over and over. Isn't that what the word habit means? Let's look at the true definition of the word *habit*. According to Merriam-Webster Online Dictionary, the word habit is, "a behavior pattern acquired by frequent repetition or an acquired mode of behavior that has become nearly or completely involuntary." [1] That is what we have been working on all this time. Developing **personal money management skills** is accomplished by using frequent repetition with the desired outcome in mind and practicing them as a normal routine, in your life, nearly or completely involuntarily. That is why it may sound like I am repeating myself, which I probably am (it's hereditary; I got it from my father who repeated himself all the time) but it is because you need to understand and completely grasp the concept of YOUR MONEY, DAY ONE to set yourself up for your financial future. It really boils down to a few basic financial concepts. And yes, they have to be repeated over and over on a consistent basis. It is exactly what the definition of the word

---

1 http://www.merriam-webster.com/

habit is. Learn and understand the concepts now, in order to benefit from them for the rest of your life. It is pretty simple, but there are millions of people out there that have yet to grasp the concepts and understand that they, too, have the ability to create a successful financial future. Don't be one of them. I applaud you for making the commitment to start developing good habits, right now.

The reason I share this with you is one, I want you to know I genuinely care about providing you with the best possible advice to help you get started on the road to your financial future. And two, the basic points of this program need to be remembered, and need to be repeated so you will master them.

That brings me to this section entitled, The **BIG 3**. What are The BIG 3? They are: *start early, be disciplined* and *have patience*. We have discussed all three of these to some extent, now let's take this opportunity to dedicate some specific time to discuss each one of them, individually, as they relate to establishing your solid foundation.

You might be asking yourself why I call these The BIG 3. Well, plain and simple **these are three very important traits for long term financial success**. You do not need to have a lot of money or need to be working in a high paying job; you don't have to be a professional like a doctor, dentist, or lawyer, nor a high paid sports star. You do not have to be categorized as any of these. You can begin right where you are building your financial future by saving and investing your money even if it is only money that is gifted to you for special occasions or your allowance.

Whether you earn it, receive it or are lucky enough to win it there are certain steps that you can follow in your life. You have the ability to totally control your money to launch you on your way. The BIG 3 are traits that will help you.

Start Early

The first trait is the one we have been repeating over and over and over: **START EARLY**. It cannot be emphasized enough how important this is. What start early really means is – time, taking advantage of one of the most precious commodities that there is. Once it is gone you can never get it back, it is like watching sand pass through an hour glass. *Start early* means establishing a savings program that will utilize time to build financial wealth. You saw firsthand what a HUGE difference it makes when we discussed it in the section called 'The Two-Headed Monster' with the multiple examples of the power of compound interest. The one thing that made ALL the difference in the investor scenarios was time. You saw the rewards of what happened when it was used to its fullest by starting early and you saw how damaging it can be when you put off saving until later. Lack of time affects your financial situation; start early, it is the key if you want to truly take establishing an investment portfolio seriously, the earlier the better. Your financial future depends on this one basic concept. It has nothing to do with how much money you have now or how much you are making now, it has to do with establishing the habit. Don't wait; do it now; start early. Time is on your side, time is your best friend right now, along with the friendly monster – compound interest; starting early is the key. When you are feeling in doubt, start early. If all else fails, start early. (By the way did I mention that I take after my dad by often repeating myself? Well – I do, I'm sorry.) **Start early**.

Be Disciplined

Now that we agree that you understand the importance of starting early and have a crystal clear understanding of why it is so important, let's look at the second trait of The BIG 3 – **BE DISCIPLINED**. Remember, it is about saving money; it is about forming habits. When you do have money, you will automatically (or as the definition stated "completely involuntarily") follow through with a behavior, saving money on a consistent and repeated basis, in order to build your savings accounts. That is what being disciplined means, always making sure that you make it a priority to set aside money in each of the specific categories discussed in the chapters on budgeting and paying yourself first. *Discipline* is really a by-product of staying focused, always maintaining a clear vision, as it relates to achieving your goals. This applies not only to your financial life, but all areas of your life; your career, your personal life, your relationships, etc. **Forming a level of discipline in your financial life can lead to many positive rewards in other areas of your life**. But like anything that requires a lot of work, it won't be easy. We never said that this was going to be easy. Discipline will also interact with that one precious commodity that keeps getting mentioned – time. It takes time to become disciplined; it is like anything you want to be good at, it takes practice. Practice takes time. Time develops habits. Forming life long habits will take a lot of effort, but the sooner you can develop the discipline, the better off you are going to be. (Oh, one last thing, did I mention that key to this whole thing is to **START EARLY**. Just thought I would drop that in again.)

Have Patience

The third and final trait of The BIG 3 is a virtue that if people could develop on a grand scale, the world would be an even more incredible place than it is. The last trait is – **HAVE PATIENCE**. There is an old saying that dates back to around the time of 1377 by a man named William Langland in the Middle English allegorical narrative poem entitled Piers Plowman (or Visio Willelmi de Petro Ploughman). Mr. Langland used the saying, "Patience is the greatest virtue." I believe that this saying is poignant, especially when it comes to developing savings habits, like the ones discussed in this program. **Patience is a virtue**. It is having perseverance, discipline, the intestinal fortitude and the outright desire to be able to take time to wait and see the fruits of your labors pay off in the long run. Practice *patience* and you will be rewarded.

Frustration

There is one thing that seems to interfere with the ability for humans to practice patience on a consistent basis and that is the emotion of frustration. When things do not go our way or as planned, we tend to lose our patience. This happens most commonly when we are not in control of a situation and the outcomes are not turning out the way in which we desire, causing us to be frustrated and resulting in our loss of patience. We tend to overreact and make rash decisions that have negative or damaging ramifications. I think this is something we can probably all relate to that has happened to us with our parents and school work, something they are trying to manage, but at the same time, counting on you to complete. Think of a time when your parent asks if a certain task is finished (one that you really should have done hours ago) and you answer, "No." The next thing you know your parent is going off on you and raising his or her voice. This is a true picture of how frustration, due to lack of complete control (unless they do your homework for you), can cause one to lose one's patience.

Frustration, followed by loss of patience can also happen when it comes to your financial situation. You learn and understand the importance of sound personal money management skills, you follow along with the program, take the advice that is given, put a conscious effort into the first two traits of The BIG 3. Then, when something negatively affects the financial world, or your accounts remain flat as a result of overall economic conditions and have not met your expectations, you become increasingly frustrated, grow impatient, (just as your parents did) and you lose it. In 'losing it,' you decide that you are going to close the account, and move the money to the 'hot' mutual fund or stock that Jim Cramer is screaming about on Mad Money (booyah). You abort your financial strategy, chasing the 'hot' mutual fund or stock and then what? By doing this you have now aborted a solid investment strategy and you have resorted to gambling with your retirement money, like placing it all on '26' at a roulette table in Las Vegas.

Stay in Your Lane

When I was a financial advisor with Paine Webber, now UBS, we used to hear something all the time, it was just about as bad as me repeating things over and over in this book. (Have I mentioned to you that you need to start early?) The story was about how investing is like driving on the freeway, constantly changing lanes to try to get ahead of the next driver so you can get where you are going quicker. Recently as I was reading an article in the Personal Finance section of the T. Rowe Price newsletter entitled, *Coping With Stock Market Volatility*,[2] it reminded me of that story.

In the article, T. Rowe Price certified financial planner, Stuart Ritter, made some excellent comments regarding the issue of people coping with market volatility, which is really just a fancy way of talking about having patience. Mr. Ritter said, "If you don't need the money for years, what the stock market does over the course of a week, month, or even several months really isn't that relevant. Investors should have their assets carved up in different ways for different purposes and time periods – higher allocations to stocks for longer-term goals and lower allocations for shorter-term goals. Attempting to time the rise and fall of stock markets or overreacting to short-term market developments is often a fruitless exercise. Investors who did not foresee this summer's turbulence are also not likely to accurately predict the right time to jump back into stocks. It's kind of like drivers who are constantly changing lanes. Their lane backs up so they switch lanes. But what invariably happens? The lane they just moved to starts backing up. And they don't get any farther down the road. Investors are generally better off sticking with a well-diversified investment strategy rather than changing lanes."

What Mr. Ritter is saying is when you have established your financial goals and you have developed an investment strategy, you should not start changing things because of short term market fluctuations. The traffic analogy is a good one as it addresses the very issue we are discussing, developing patience. Yes, the other lane may appear to be moving faster, that latest 'hot' mutual fund is performing miraculously, but then when you switch to the next lane and sell out of your mutual fund to buy the new one, you notice that the car in the other lane, your previous mutual fund, begins performing well again. Switching back and forth is not a sound strategy. That is why I say that when you establish a mutual fund account, choose one that has a long history of weathering the storm of economic fluctuations in the market. Stay in your lane and let the traffic flow. Develop patience

---

2 "Coping with Stock Market Volatility." T. Rowe Price Report Fall 2007: Issue no. 97. T. Rowe Price Investment Services, Inc. Distributors 2007

– let it be your friend. Develop friendships with each of the BIG 3, just as you develop real life friendships; they can be rewarding and satisfying. It will not be rosy all the time, because friendships have their ups and downs, but in the long run those valuable friendships are worth it.

By developing the third trait of The BIG 3 – patience – you will be able to handle future situations that will arise, not just when it comes to your financial situations, but your life situations as well. **Developing patience will help you to deal with the frustrations that can impede your decision making process, thus assisting you to be successful in your life**. Just remember this, "The ability to wait for something without excessive frustration is a valuable character trait." That says it all, doesn't it?

Once again, we have covered a lot of important and valuable information. The BIG 3 are very easy to remember, *start early, be disciplined* and *have patience*. But as simple as they may seem, they are very difficult to master. In order to do so, it will take a lot of hard work and a level of commitment on your part, to continue to journey down the path that will lead you to your financial goals. You have done an AWESOME job staying with this chapter and all the previous ones for that matter. I both applaud and commend you for your focused attention. Let's move on.

Chapter 14

THE EIGHT KEY POINTS TO INVESTING

With extensive experience in the real world, I have witnessed the way it has significantly changed over time and it is clear to me why in today's world time is so scarce and valuable. The lives of young adults have so much going on, far more than I ever had at that age. With all the technological advances including computers, cell phones, the internet, video game systems, cable television and much more, successfully managing all the demands is challenging. After you have completed this program it is highly unlikely that you will go back and review it in its entirety. That's okay; I would be flattered if you did, but its okay if you don't. My experience with young adults and how well I've come to know them (remember, I have a 22 year old daughter, Megan, and a 15 year old stepson, Michael, not to mention the many students I interact with every day) helps me understand the challenges they face managing time. I am sure at times it feels like the old saying 'it's a rat race,' like watching laboratory rats running in a spinning wheel – going so fast but never really getting anywhere. As I have stated before, I sincerely want to help young adults successfully develop the necessary habits that will lead to sound personal money management skills.

That is why I have developed **The Eight Key Points to Investing**. This will give you a resource upon which you can draw to refresh your memory from time to time. Cutting to the chase; this chapter will provide an abbreviated version of the key points to developing the habits necessary for sound personal money management skills and to begin building your future investment portfolio.

Let's review the eight key points that you need to know when it comes to saving money for retirement. Here we go!

Point #1: Start Early

Starting as early as possible is the key when it comes to building a savings program. As it was discussed in the section, 'The Two-Headed Monster,' time is the most important factor as it relates to taking full advantage of compound interest. Time has an incredible effect on your money and your future.

Point #2: Be Disciplined

Nothing in life comes easily. There is nothing that better describes the true meaning of taking personal responsibility of your financial situation than being 'disciplined.' It requires an immense amount of personal fortitude and a level of perseverance second to none. It requires you to make a conscious decision to develop personal money management skills by establishing an investment portfolio that will ultimately provide for your financial future. The reason discipline will be so important, but hard at the same time, is that word we talked about earlier – temptation. You are going to be faced with many temptations, demands, needs, wants – whatever you might call them – that will literally zap the money right out of your hands. But that is why we discussed, in detail, the need to form the habits that will set you up for success. Set up a budget by which to live. Learn and understand what 'paying yourself first' means. Understand what it means to take the personal responsibility to devote some time to charting a course that you will follow. The few years of short term discomfort will be far outweighed by the long term gains of a solid financial future. Your biggest challenge will be to resist temptation, not to succumb to peer pressure and to take control of your life in a manner that will benefit you for years to come.

Point #3: Have Patience

To have patience is to gain a complete understanding of how important time is in establishing a solid foundation for you to build your financial portfolio. We saw it firsthand in the section 'The Two-Headed Monster.' Patience is about allowing yourself enough time to take advantage of all the financial tools available over a series of years. Time is the most precious commodity, we know that, and using it correctly can set you up for financial success. Like the example of being in traffic and watching the cars around you move ahead, you can become frustrated and want to switch lanes, which can steer you off course. Don't give in to the feeling of frustration. Stay focused on your long term goals. Have patience. Remember, patience is a virtue; practice it.

Point #4: Understand and Research Mutual Funds

A mutual fund is an investment in which a financial company takes your money and other investors' money, pools it together forming a group of investors and then buys stocks in companies for the fund that will meet the goals and objectives of the fund. The money is invested in a diversified manner among a group, or portfolio, of different companies.

Mutual funds offer a wide variety of options to investors, especially when your investment amount may be limited to begin with. That flexibility provides the freedom to establish a savings program, without putting a strain on your personal financial situation. The other key advantage of owning mutual funds is that they offer diversification (not placing all your eggs in one basket) and a dedicated professional money manager whose sole purpose is to insure that the mutual fund follows the objectives set forth and performs positively for its investors.

There are literally thousands of types of mutual funds available. They all have different investment objectives and goals and have different levels of risks and diversity within them. You will see funds that have names like large-cap, mid-cap, and small-cap which will invest in companies of various sizes within the portfolio. There are funds called sector funds that invest primarily in one type of business such as financial companies, technology companies or health care and pharmaceutical companies.

Research individual mutual funds, specifically large cap growth funds. Since you are young, you should consider being more aggressive early on, researching and analyzing mutual funds that you will find in the large cap 'blue chip' funds that primarily hold large companies competing in the global economy, including names like Microsoft, Google, Target, Cisco Systems, Apple and General Electric just to name a few. Companies within this fund classification will have potential for long-term growth, they will be trying to grow more than other companies within their sector and they strive for profit growth. Establishing this type of mutual fund will serve as your foundation as you move forward in building a financial portfolio.

However, you must research and analyze the type of mutual fund with which you will begin investing. One common variable that you can look at to be able to compare apples to apples is called a Morningstar rating. Just knowing about the basics of Morningstar will help you when you are researching mutual funds or communicating with an investment professional.

Point #5: Know the Level of Risk

When an investment company establishes a mutual fund, it will set up the fund according to a certain investment objective or strategy. That is why there are so many funds offered to assist individual investors in developing diversified investment portfolios to match their needs. There are various ways that you will see mutual fund companies express the levels of risk. The most common terms that you can look for are aggressive, moderate and conservative. You may also see levels of risk described in the manner of high, medium or low. Remember, the higher the average price fluctuations the higher the risk and the lower the average price fluctuations the lower the risk.

Point #6: Obtain and Read the Prospectus and Report Information

EVERY mutual fund will have a prospectus. **You must obtain a prospectus before purchasing any investment**. It can be either requested from the brokerage company or mutual fund company or downloaded from the internet. If you are using a brokerage company with a financial representative or broker, they will also be able to provide it to you upon request. The prospectus is one of the most valuable pieces of information available to investors. It describes, *in detail*, everything that an investor needs to know in order to make an educated and wise decision. It will go into detail about the level of risk, fees and expenses and the past performance. **There is one important thing to always remember about mutual funds, past performance will not guarantee future results**. It will also contain some very important information pertaining to the minimum amount of money that will be needed to open the account and the guidelines that will go along with it. **You should never invest any money without reading the prospectus first**.

Also request or download the most recent quarterly report or annual report. These reports will contain the most current and up to date information on how the fund is performing and also explain how the current stock market conditions have been affecting the activity and performance of the fund.

Point #7: Open a Mutual Fund Account

After deciding on the fund of your choice, contact the company and request the necessary information to open a mutual fund account. Request the paperwork needed to create an automatic transfer that will automatically move the desired amount of money that you want to invest each and every month from your checking or savings account to the mutual fund account. Speak with someone on the telephone, the customer service representatives are *extremely* helpful. Or if it is convenient for you to go to an office of an investment company, take advantage of the experience.

The way to get started with what will eventually become your investment portfolio, will depend on your personal situation. (It sounds so serious and pretentious, doesn't it? Like something you would say while attending a fancy dinner.)

If you are 18 or over, you are eligible to open a brokerage account under your own name. If you are under the age of 18, you will need to talk to your parent(s) or guardian(s) about helping you set one up. This will involve some additional paperwork, but it will be worth it to take advantage of time. These guardian or custodial accounts are called ***Uniform Gifts to Minors Act (UGMA)*** or the ***Uniform Transfers to Minors Act (UTMA)***. They are set up with the parent or guardian as a joint owner of the account. Once the minor turns 18 and becomes of legal age the account can be properly converted so the minor now becomes the sole owner. There are different ways of setting up who will be responsible for any taxes you may incur, but it is usually advantageous to have the minor own the assets since the tax rate will typically be lower because of the minor's lower annual income. This is another one of those times that contacting a tax advisor may be beneficial.

Once you get to this point, as simple and basic as it may appear, you are far ahead of the majority of people in planning for your financial future.

Point #8: Follow Major Stock Market Indexes and Track Your Investments

After you go through all the work of setting up accounts, filling out paperwork, getting everything ready, and you begin to make deposits, the one additional thing that you should do is take interest in following the economic conditions of the world. This is not about tracking what your fund has done each minute or hour of the day or even daily because remember you are focused on the long term. The easiest way to track your mutual fund is to look it up online. You can use the mutual fund company's website or you can use a financial website such as Morningstar, Yahoo Finance, MarketWatch.com or TheStreet.com. (TheStreet.com site is very user friendly and offers a comprehensive snap shot of the fund's performance.) In order to access the information, there will be a box, located on the site, where the ticker symbol is entered. Here is an example of the type of information that you will find:

Mutual Fund Name – the name of the mutual fund and the mutual fund company.

Ticker Symbol – the specific symbol associated with the fund.

Net Asset Value (NAV) – the price at the close of the business day.

Change – the amount the NAV has changed (increased or decreased) from the day before. This number may be expressed as a dollar figure and/or a percentage.

Previous Close or Previous NAV - the dollar value of a share from the day before.

Previous NAV Date – the last date the mutual fund was priced.

YTD Return – the year to date rate of return, expressed in a percentage, for the performance of the fund.

The following is an example of what the above information may look like for a mutual fund:

Large Cap Growth Fund	**AMCDX**
NAV	17.36
Change	+ 0.80 | 4.83%
Previous Close	16.56
Previous NAV Date	06/05/08
YTD Return	6.26%

While it is not necessary to look at this information on a daily basis, it is useful to understand it so when you do take a look at your mutual fund you will be able to decipher the performance of the fund in a quick and efficient manner. Also remember that you will be receiving periodic information (in the mail and/or electronically) pertaining to the performance of the fund, in addition to tracking it yourself.

You do not have to be an investment guru, but take a look each day at the major stock market indexes, the Dow Jones Industrial Average, the S&P 500, the NASDAQ, etc. to stay informed of the general state of economic business conditions and what effect they are having on the stock markets.

There you have it. The eight key points that you need to establish a long-term savings program that you will build upon as you move into your adult life. This is the condensed version, all the background information is important for you to be able to understand it. Review this from time to time and keep it fresh in your mind, it will help keep you focused, and on track with the habits needed for your financial future. We're getting there; we can see the light at the end of the tunnel. Let's move forward.

Chapter 15

QUICKSTART GUIDE

Belie it or not you have made it to the last chapter of this book. I know there has been an incredible amount of information covered and at times I am sure you thought it would never end. But it is almost over. This now brings us to the point in which I want to provide you with an easy reference tool called a QuickStart Guide. **The QuickStart Guide is designed to provide you with a concise yet thorough step by step process to take all the information we have discussed and make an action plan to implement it into your life.** When you need a clearer understanding or a refresher course regarding a specific topic, go back to the chapter and review it in its entirety. The QuickStart Guide is to be used to complement the detailed information, giving you a summary of the necessary steps to get you started TODAY on your path to developing sound personal money management skills.

QuickStart Guide

QS #1   Go to a bank and open a checking account with a debit card.

(If you are under the age of 18, you will need to have a parent or guardian with you.) When you open an account become familiar with your **account number** and also understand the **ABA (American Banker's Association) Routing Number**. It will be necessary to have a minimum of $100-$150 to open an account.

Sample Check

Tracy and Lisa Ferguson	01-23/4567	1000
1234 Austin Road		
Homewood, IL 56789		_____20____
Pay to the		
Order of _____	$ _____	
_____		Dollars
Anywhere Bank		
Anywhere City		
Memo_____	_____	
|:02100100|: 010112020 01000		

ABA Routing Number   Account Number   Check Number

At the same time also open a separate savings account(s) so that you may begin making the monthly transfers of the 10% that we discussed in the budgeting section of this program. Remember, this will be used for establishing a retirement fund, an emergency and/or a planned purchases fund and a charity or giving fund. You will need a minimum of $50 to open an account.

If you are already employed, go to QS #3

QS #2   Begin earning money.

If you are still in high school, get permission from your parents. This will entail getting a part-time job of no more than 20 hours per week. If you are not in high school, get a job that will fit your current schedule. Understand and review all the information pertaining to your paycheck. Make sure it is accurate and correct.

QS #3   Establish a budget.

Utilize the worksheets provided and complete the information to form your budget. Begin managing your money and achieving your financial goals. Develop the habit of paying yourself first. Begin setting aside money in the three suggested categories; 10% for retirement, 10% for savings/emergency fund and 10% for charity. *This is an extremely important habit to form.*

QS #4   Utilize the eight key points to investing.

This includes opening a mutual fund account and developing sound financial habits that will lead to developing a successful investment strategy.

QS #5   Understand and effectively manage credit card debt.

Implement and practice money management skills to eliminate your dependence on using plastic. Remember the other head of the Two-Headed Monster.

QS #6   Review financial account information.

Take the time each month to review your financial accounts. Review the information for accuracy and consistency. It is your responsibility to take control of your personal financial situation.

QS #7   Maintain neat and thorough financial records.

This is a very important habit to form and perfectly complements developing sound personal money management skills. Be organized in your financial life.

QS #8   Know how to file a tax return and why.

This aspect of your financial life is not centered on one day. This is an extremely important responsibility. Certain financial decisions that are made over a twelve month period become an integral part of your financial situation. Most decisions made can only be changed not corrected. This is one habit where utilizing a tax professional could be invaluable.

QS #9   Continue to practice The BIG 3:

START EARLY – utilize the most precious commodity there is – time.

BE DISCIPLINED – remain focused, have a clear vision of your goals.

HAVE PATIENCE – keep in mind your long term goals and don't be frustrated by short term market fluctuations; stay in your lane.

QS #10   Become a life long learner.

It is important for you to continue to seek out current and up-to-date information. No matter where you live, you will always have access to a major newspaper and if not, at least read the local paper in your area EVERY DAY. It won't just keep you informed and up-to-date about what is happening in the business world and the overall economic conditions surrounding it, but it will also keep you informed about the world in which you live as a whole. Along with reading a newspaper, I would strongly suggest subscribing to a monthly financial periodical such as Kiplinger's Personal Finance Magazine, SmartMoney Magazine or Money Magazine. All are excellent personal financial resources that will educate you on key issues and assist you in further understanding the concepts that we have discussed.

Well, there you have it, the QuickStart Guide. A concise summary of what it will take for you to get started. Take some time and move down the list, one by one, following the path to your financial future. Let's move on to my closing thoughts.

CLOSING THOUGHTS

We have covered a lot of information together since we started. While I was planning and working on this book I was very cognizant of keeping this experience unlike a lecture from your parents or a situation in which you are listening to someone droning on and on and you just want to be put out of your misery. I wanted to take what I believe is some of the most important information that you will need in your life and make it both enjoyable and fun while at the same time a valuable learning experience. This is not just a job for me, this is my passion. My passion is to convert financial concepts into information that is easily understandable for young adults to help them carve out a path to a successful financial future. I hope that I have achieved this goal and you have gotten that message from me. As we part ways, I want to take this opportunity to leave you with some closing thoughts.

It is important for you to understand that to have a financial future that will meet all of your needs, wants and desires, it is going to take hard work. It is going to take dedication, perseverance, discipline and an outright mindset for you to establish the successful habits that will set you on your course. When I started out on this project I intended this book to be about helping young adults save money for retirement. I want young adults to have an opportunity to learn the basics of establishing both successful money management habits and skills, to be able to understand what saving and investing is all about, so when it is time to participate in a 401(k) they will know exactly what to do. They won't be like so many people today, those with such a lack of knowledge about investing, that they have to be automatically enrolled in their programs, with choices made for them. I do not want this to be you. I want you to control your money.

The farther I got into it and the more I thought about it, saving for retirement was an important, but small part of it. It became much more than that. It is about developing a financial lifestyle, like when people develop a healthy living lifestyle by making decisions to alter or change their eating habits, eating more fruits and vegetables, cutting out high fat foods and beginning an exercise regiment. It is about making a conscious decision to live your life a certain way. We talked about the importance of starting at an early age and continuing all the way into your 'golden years.' We did it in a variety of ways. All the topics are related and woven into each other. By practicing them as part of your life you will be able to experience the financial lifestyle you want and deserve.

I hope that this book is not something that you will close and place on your shelf to collect dust. When you successfully achieve the points we discussed and you are living the habits of a new financial lifestyle it will be okay for you to do that. But until then, keep it handy, use it as a reference and as you have children, share your insight and practice it with them. At the very least you can practice a saying that my friend, Laurie, instilled in me a long time ago; take what you like and leave the rest. Use what you need to develop your own personal money management skills to be financially successful.

What I really hope you learn from me is this: it is your responsibility to take care of your own personal financial situation and you will only get one shot at it. So instead of learning the hard way, by the 'school of hard knocks,' do it the right way. Practice the habit of living a responsible financial lifestyle and properly managing your money. Understand that you are young now, but you are going to age day by day, year by year and before you know it you are going to be in your golden years. Take advantage of one of the most precious commodities there is – time. START EARLY (there I go again repeating myself) taking advantage of time and compound interest; it will put you on your path. While you are working so hard to earn, save and manage money, STAY OUT OF DEBT. Do not fall prey to giving your money away in interest when you could be saving it. (If you need to be reminded go back to the comparison example we discussed between paying credit interest vs. earning it.) It is your money and you certainly do not want to put yourself in a financial position that is going to add pressure to your life.

Young adults express to me all the time that they can't wait to be on their own. I always say don't be in such a hurry, the real world isn't all it's cracked up to be. The real world is a hard place and having money issues and problems on top of it will certainly not make it better.

Live your passion, whatever it is and don't let ANYONE get in the way. Take responsibility for your financial future. It is your hard earned money; take control of it or it will take control of you.

I have thoroughly enjoyed this experience and hope you have as well. Please feel free to share your success stories with me as there is nothing I will enjoy more. You can reach me at www.michaeljwagner.net. I wish you all the best and thank you for reading this book. Take care.

Mr. Wagner
Los Angeles, CA USA

GLOSSARY

-A-

ABA Routing Number – The number in the lower left hand corner of a check. It is used to identify the financial institution upon which the check is drawn. This number is used for both the sorting and clearing of checks as well as conducting electronic transactions such as direct deposits or automatic transfers. **p. 32, 170**

Account Fee – The amount charged for maintenance of an account. **p. 90**

Account Number – A number or series of numbers that is assigned to an accountholder. **p. 170**

Aggressive (High) – A level of risk that is associated with above average market or price fluctuations and seeks higher rates of returns. **p. 78**

American Express – A global financial services company that offers a variety of both personal and business financial services. Most commonly known for the American Express Card. **p. 65**

Annual Percentage Rate – The interest rate, expressed as a percentage, which indicates the total cost, including all fees, of a particular credit transaction. It is a way to standardize the disclosure of an interest rate in order to make it easier for the consumer to compare similar transactions. **p. 128**

ATM (Automated Teller Machine) – A machine that allows access to money by using credit cards, debit cards or ATM cards, 24 hours a day. **p. 7**

Automatic Investment Plan – Money that is deposited to an account automatically on a repeated basis, e.g. weekly, monthly, quarterly. This is normally done as an automatic transfer from a bank account or as a deduction from a paycheck. **p. 91**

Automatic Reinvestment – An option a mutual fund owner has of investing dividend income and capital gains distributions back into their mutual fund account. This works like compound interest. **p. 83**

Average Annual Total Return – The performance of a fund expressed as a percentage, of the overall performance for all years figured into an average. **p. 81**

-B-

Bank – A financial institution that offers a wide variety of financial products and services for both personal and business purposes, including checking and savings accounts. **p. 8**

Bankruptcy – The legal process in which an individual is declared incapable of paying debts and obligations to those owed money. This will also be recorded on a credit report and will remain on it for many years. It will be extremely difficult to obtain future credit. **p. 74, 129**

Bond Fund – A mutual fund that is primarily comprised of investments that earn income. These funds are typically made up of investments surrounding municipal, corporate, or US government bonds. **p. 79**

Broker/Stockbroker – An employee of a financial services company who will provide investment advice as well as assist in buying and selling investment products and services. (Also known as an Investment Advisor) **p. 87, 88**

Budgeting – A formalized plan to control spending by utilizing the money one earns or has available (income), and prioritizing the money one spends (expenses) on a monthly basis. **p. 40, 42, 125**

-C-

Cash – Money carried to make purchases. **p. 6**

Certificate of Deposit (CD) – An investment in which money is deposited into an account for a certain length of time (term), with a specific maturity date at a certain interest rate. Typically the longer the length of time (term) the higher the rate of interest earned. If the funds are withdrawn before the maturity date there may be an interest penalty. **p. 10**

Charge Card – A plastic card that is issued by a retail business, e.g. department store, that enables the accountholder to purchase goods and then pay for them at a later date, with interest. **p. 63**

Checking Account – An account held at a financial institution. Funds are deposited by the accountholder and also withdrawn by writing a check or electronically by using a debit card or automatically by the use of an automatic transfer. **p. 8**

Company Matching Program – The money contributed to an employee's account as part a 401(k) retirement program. This is a benefit offered as part of a compensation package. Matching contributions are made either by a dollar amount or a percentage of the employee's contribution. **p. 27**

Compound Interest – Interest earned on an investment. The interest is then added to the account balance and interest is then earned on the new balance, thus earning interest on interest. This increases the value of an investment over time. **p. 104**

Conservative (Low) – A level of risk that is associated with little or no market or price fluctuations and typically seeks lower rates of returns. **p. 78**

Credit Card – A plastic card that is issued by a financial institution, bank or business, that enables the accountholder to purchase goods and services and then pay for them at a later date, with interest. **p. 13**

Credit Rating – An evaluation of a person's performance in handling money as a result of paying their bills and obligations on time. The credit rating is converted into a number, known as a FICO score. The number determines an individual's credit worthiness to anyone considering extending credit. The higher the score the better the credit history. **p. 129**

Credit Report – A file that is maintained by credit reporting agencies showing your payment history on all credit or borrowing accounts. It may also contain legal action that has been filed against you such as bankruptcy, liens, judgments, etc. **p. 129**

-D-

Debit Card – A plastic card that is issued by a financial institution, which enables the accountholder to purchase goods and services by automatically withdrawing money from a bank account electronically. It can also be used at an ATM to withdraw money. **p. 12**

Debt – Money that is owed for goods and/or services purchased and is required to be paid at a later date. **p. 17, 122**

Deduction(s) – Items that are subtracted from gross pay. **p. 25**

Deferred Sales Charge – The amount charged when selling shares of a mutual fund. **p. 86**

Defined Contribution Plan – See 401(k) **p. 27, 182**

Direct Deposit – Money that is electronically deposited into a financial account, e.g. checking or savings account. Popular transactions include paychecks and tax refunds. **p. 31**

Discipline – Developing a behavior, while focused on a goal, by establishing a habit that will yield a positive result. **p. 67, 156**

Discount Brokerage Company – A financial company that offers investment products and services with lower fees and commissions than a full service brokerage company. It does not give advice regarding the purchase of specific investments to an investor. **p. 88**

Discover – One of the top four credit cards in the United States with over 50 million cardholders. Originally issued in 1985. **p. 66**

Distribution Fees (12b–1) – Fees associated with the advertising and promotional costs of a mutual fund. Expenses include the marketing and selling of shares, advertising, sales literature, compensation for brokers and printing and mailing of literature. A complete description of fees will be disclosed in the fund's prospectus. **p. 90**

Diversification – Establishing a variety of investments that have varying goals, objectives and risk tolerance. This is what the old adage "do not place all your eggs in one basket" means. **p. 74**

Dollar Cost Averaging – The habit of investing a fixed dollar amount in an investment (such as a mutual fund) on a regular basis for a long period of time. Doing so should reduce the average share cost by purchasing more shares in the fund when the NAV (Net Asset Value) is lower and purchasing fewer shares when the NAV is higher. **p. 99**

Donation – A gift of either time or money given to a favorite charity, supporting a specific cause or institution without receiving anything in return. **p. 38**

Domestic Stock Fund – A mutual fund that invests primarily in U.S. companies. **p. 79**

Dow Jones Industrial Average – An index that is made up of 30 of the most actively traded 'blue chip' stocks. The index provides an indication of the overall condition of the United States stock market and is most commonly used in reporting the day's overall performance. **p. 84**

-E-

Earned Money – Money that is received from wages earned from either performing work or working at a job as an employee of a business. **p. 2**

Earnings Statement – A document containing a summary of payroll information, both current and year to date, for an individual. **p. 23**

Easy Money – Money that is given to you by your parents, relatives, friends, etc. **p. 1**

Emergency Fund – Money that is set aside to be used to cover unexpected expenses. **p. 55**

Expense Ratio – See Total Annual Fund Operating Expenses. **p. 90, 187**

-F-

Federal Income Tax – The amount of money that is withheld or levied by the federal government from gross pay. **p. 25, 135**

Fees – An amount of money paid for a service. **p. 15, 90**

FINRA (Financial Industry Regulatory Authority) – The largest non–governmental regulator of all securities firms doing business in the United States. FINRA is dedicated to investor protection and market integrity through effective and efficient regulation, complementary compliance and technology–based services. **p. 94**

Fixed Expenses – Items paid on a repeated basis, monthly, quarterly or annually. The dollar amount of the expense may or may not remain the same. **p. 44**

401(k) – A tax deferred retirement program established by an employer which allows employees to set aside part of their salary or wages for retirement on a pre–tax basis. It is also commonly referred to as a defined contribution plan. **p. 27**

403(b) – A tax deferred retirement program, similar to the 401(k), but designed specifically for employees of schools, universities, charitable and non–profit organizations. **p. 26**

Free – Receiving something without having to pay for it. **p. 19**

Full Service Brokerage Company – A financial company that offers investment products and services, as well as investment advice and assesses sales charges and commissions. **p. 85**

Fund Classification – The type or classification of a mutual fund, e.g. Growth, Bond, Income, etc. **p. 79**

-G-

Gifted Money – Money that is received from special events in one's life or certain life situations such as an inheritance. **p. 2**

Golden Years – The period of time of living in retirement. **p. 70, 120**

Gross Pay – The amount of money earned BEFORE any deductions are subtracted. **p. 21, 24**

-H-

Habit – A behavior that is developed and repeated either voluntarily or involuntarily. **p. 154**

-I-

Index Fund – A mutual fund designed to track the performance of a specific stock market index and to create a portfolio of specific stocks similar to that of the index. For example the S&P 500 Index. (S&P stands for Standard and Poor's.) **p. 79**

Individual Retirement Account (IRA) – An investment account for individuals that offers tax deferred savings for retirement. **p. 29, 97**

Industry Holdings – Companies that comprise a specific business sector in the portfolio of investments within a mutual fund. **p. 76**

Insurance Company – A business that offers a variety of financial products and services to both businesses and individuals. **p. 86**

Interest – The amount of money that is *earned* from saving money or the amount of money that is *paid* for borrowing money. **p. 9**

Interest Rate – The rate that is earned on money being saved or the rate that is charged to borrow money. **p. 83**

International Fund – A mutual fund that invests primarily in companies outside the U.S. **p. 79**

Investment Advisor – An employee of a financial services company who will provide investment advice as well as assist in buying and selling investment products and services. (Also known as Broker/ Stockbroker) **p. 75**

Investment Goal – The intended quantity and purpose of money being saved. **p. 77**

Investment Objective – The specific goal a mutual fund is trying to achieve. An objective can include growth of capital, growth of income, growth & income, current income, or preserve capital, just to name a few. **p. 80**

IRS (Internal Revenue Service) – The federal agency of the United States government that is responsible for properly collecting federal income taxes in the United States. The IRS is responsible for administering and enforcing the laws, policies and procedures of the United States Treasury Department. **p. 135**

-L-

Large–Cap Growth Fund – A mutual fund that is comprised of large established 'blue chip' companies with over $10 billion in market capitalization. **p. 80**

Lipper Index – An index service that analyzes mutual fund performance, as it relates to funds similar to that of its peers or sectors. **p. 82**

-M-

Management Fee – The amount of money that is paid out of the mutual fund to the fund or portfolio manager for overseeing the fund. A complete description of the fee will be disclosed in the funds prospectus. **p. 90**

MasterCard – One of the top four credit cards in the United States, originally issued in 1967. **p. 65**

Medicare Tax – A deduction from a paycheck that is used to provide medical benefits for individuals after the age of 65. **p. 26**

Mid–Cap Growth Fund – A mutual fund that is comprised of medium sized companies with between $2 billion and $10 billion in market capitalization. **p. 80**

Minimum Payment – The smallest monthly payment amount accepted by a creditor. **p. 123**

Moderate (Medium) – A level of risk that is associated with average market and price fluctuations to pursue higher returns. **p. 78**

Money Market Fund – A mutual fund comprised of investments such as money market securities, certificates of deposit (CDs), U.S. Government securities such as T–Bills, repurchase agreements, commercial paper, etc., that is classified as a relatively safe investment. **p. 79**

Morningstar – An independent research firm that compares performance results of mutual funds against funds of a similar nature. Uses a five star rating system, 5 is excellent and 1 is poor. **p. 82**

Mutual Fund – An investment product that brings together money from many people to be invested. The fund manager selects and organizes certain investments (a portfolio), which meets the overall objective of the fund. Each investor owns shares and becomes a shareholder. **p. 74**

-N-

NASDAQ (National Association of Securities Dealers Automated Quotations) – An electronic stock exchange that is made up of 3,300 companies. Companies listed on the NASDAQ are primarily new, have high growth potential and also can be considered volatile. The NASDAQ provides an indication of the overall condition of a segment of the United States stock market and is commonly used in reporting the day's overall performance. **p. 85**

Net Asset Value (NAV) – The end of the day market value of an individual share in a mutual fund. This is the price paid for a single share. When purchasing shares the price will be calculated on what is called 'forward pricing.' If funds are purchased in the morning, the mutual fund share price will not be determined until the price is calculated at the close of the trading day. **p. 82, 100, 167**

Net Pay – The amount of pay received after all deductions have been subtracted. **p. 21, 24**

No Sales Charge (No–Load) – A mutual fund that does not charge a sales commission or sales charge (load) when buying or selling shares. (No load does not mean that it is free of expenses associated with operating the account.) **p. 86**

-P-

Patience – Understanding the importance of time and resisting the urge to make rash decisions, while remaining focused on an established goal. **p. 73, 157**

Paycheck – A official document that an employee receives from an employer to be paid for performing work. **p. 21**

Portfolio – A collection of investments such as mutual funds, stocks, bonds, money market accounts, gold and real estate owned by an individual or organization. **p. 75**

Pre–Tax Dollars – Money for deductions that are subtracted from gross pay before tax has been calculated for withholding. **p. 30**

Prospectus – The official document produced by an investment company describing, in detail, the specifics of a mutual fund to prospective investors. The information contained in a prospectus is required by the SEC (Securities and Exchange Commission) and will consist of the fund's investment objective, strategy, risk level, fees and expenses, how to buy and sell shares, the fund manager and other essential information to assist a potential investor. **p. 91**

-R-

Rainy Day – Living in retirement years. **p. 70**

Refund Money – Money that is received from a tax refund. **p. 2, 147**

Retirement Savings Calculator – An automated program that will estimate how much money an investor will need to save for retirement based on selected criteria. **p. 72**

Risk – The level of tolerance associated with market and price fluctuations. **p. 78**

Roth IRA – An individual retirement account that offers tax free growth and allows an accountholder to have penalty free withdrawals along with tax free distributions, if certain requirements are met. **p. 98**

Rule of 72 – A simple mathematical calculation of determining the length of time it will take an investment to double at a particular compounding interest rate. **p. 83**

-S-

Sales Charge (Load) – The amount charged for an investor to buy or sell shares of a mutual fund. **p. 86**

Save – Setting money aside for future use. **p. 16**

Savings Account – An account maintained at a financial institution that pays interest on deposited funds. **p. 8, 36**

Sector Fund – A fund comprised of companies from a similar industry or market segment e.g. technology, pharmaceutical, consumer goods, medical equipment, etc. **p. 79**

Securities and Exchange Commission (SEC) – The independent United States Government regulatory agency that oversees and regulates the securities industry. **p. 94**

Share(s) – An individual unit (a stock) representing ownership in a company or organization. **p. 75**

Share Classes – Different classifications of ownership in a mutual fund. Each is set up to charge different fees based upon the class. Classes are typically 'A', 'B' or 'C.' The difference among them is in the load (either front or back end), and the fees associated with the fund. Each will have different performance results. A complete description of the classes will be disclosed in the fund's prospectus. **p. 86**

Small–Cap Growth Fund – A mutual fund comprised of small sized companies with less than $2 billion in market capitalization. **p. 80**

Social Security Tax (FICA) – The amount of money withheld from gross pay and used by the Social Security Administration to provide retirement benefits to individuals. **p. 26**

Standard & Poor's 500 (S&P 500) – An index that is made up of 500 stocks of major companies selected by market size, industry and liquidity. The index provides an indication of the overall condition of the United States stock market and is commonly used in reporting the day's overall performance. It consists of 400 industrial firms, 40 financial firms, 20 transportation firms and 40 utilities. **p. 84**

Start Early – Establishing a savings program, at a young age, that will utilize time to build financial wealth. **p. 89, 155**

State Income Tax – The amount of money that is withheld or levied by a state from gross pay. **p. 26, 148**

Stock – An individual unit (a share), defined as a certificate, representing ownership in a company or organization. **p. 76**

-T-

Target Date Funds – A mutual fund that has a mix of investments, typically other mutual funds, that normally coincides with a specific expected retirement date (these funds are also known as balanced or asset allocation funds). **p. 79**

Tax Return – A financial procedure done annually utilizing forms from the Internal Revenue Service and most states. Individuals and businesses report to the government (federal and/or state) the proper calculation of income tax. **p. 139**

Taxes – Money that is required to be paid to federal, state and local governments, to be used for goods and services under the guidelines of federal, state and local laws. **p. 25**

Temptation – A desire for something that is not necessarily needed. **p. 61**

Ticker Symbol – A company's stock or mutual fund identified by an abbreviation of letters used for trading. **p. 167**

Time – The most precious commodity used in taking full advantage of compound interest to build financial wealth. **p. 18, 70**

Time Horizon – The length of time that funds are going to be invested until they are to be withdrawn. **p. 78**

Total Annual Fund Operating Expenses – The summation of expenses associated with a mutual fund. **p. 90**

-U-

Unexpected Expenses – Money one is required to pay for unplanned expenses. (Also see Emergency Fund.) **p. 56, 181**

Uniform Gift to Minors Act (UGMA) – Legislation established in most states that allows a parent or guardian to be a custodian for financial accounts that are in a minor's name. The minor gains control of the account upon becoming of legal age, unless otherwise indicated. **p. 166**

Uniform Transfers to Minors Act (UTMA) – This is an extension of the Uniform Gift to Minors Act. Legislation established in most states that allows a parent or guardian to be a custodian for financial accounts that are in a minor's name. The minor gains control of the accounts upon becoming of legal age, unless otherwise directed. **p. 166**

Universal Default Rate – The rate of interest that an accountholder is charged when a creditor is notified of the default status of an accountholder with another creditor. The new interest rate can be adjusted to a much higher rate. **p. 128**

-V-

Variable (Optional) Expenses – Items that are not mandatory purchases and may be classified as temptations or wants. **p. 45**

Variable Default Rate – The rate of interest that an accountholder is charged after a missed or late payment. This interest rate will usually be adjusted to a much higher rate. **p. 128**

Visa – A major credit card and one of the top four credit cards in the United States. **p. 65**

-W-

W–2 Form – Wage and Tax Statement – A summary of deductions that have been withheld from wages for the year. A W–2 is legally required to be provided to the employee by January 31st of the calendar year following the previous tax year. **p. 32, 137**

W–4 Form – Employee's Withholding Allowance – An IRS form that directs an employer to withhold the correct amount of Federal and State income tax from wages. **p. 136**

-Z-

Zero – The amount of credit card debt one should have. **p. 17**

ACKNOWLEDGEMENT

After you live life, as I have for 49 years, it is difficult to be able to put together all the people you want to thank and acknowledge for making everything in your life possible. When I sat down and really began thinking about it, it is like anything else; you see those recurring moments through your mind's eye. First and foremost, I would like to thank my parents, because without them I would not have been able to do what I have done and what I wanted to do. (Plus, let's face it without being born, none of this would be possible for any of us right?) I would like to thank my older brothers Tom and Dave. They are the ones that beat me up all the time, and called me names and used to say "you're just going to be a mommy's boy." But I thank them because doing all those things made me resilient; they helped me deal with adversity and taught me how to persevere and believe in myself. Thanks, you guys!

I would like to thank both of my football coaches who taught me about the real world in different ways. (I will say one thing that they both had in common, they were excellent at yelling my name.) Thanks, Don Fox, for being an incredible 'life' teacher which prepared me to handle the real world, especially leaving that protective cocoon called 'home' after 18 years. You are a great friend and I hope you realize how you were an unbelievable influence in my life. My other coach, unfortunately will not read what I have written, but I can only hope that he is looking down over my shoulder from up above. The man I am speaking of is Stan Sheriff, my college football coach at Northern Iowa. I can still remember the day, standing at the end of the field in the UNI-Dome, all of my teammates bent over, gasping for a breath of oxygen, some even vomiting in the drains nearby. It was by far the hardest sports practice I have ever endured. He came with that stoic walk, a 'certain swagger' you could say. A pack of Benson and Hedges in his shirt pocket with a lit one in his hand, smoke bellowed from his mouth like a freight train picking up speed as he made his way to where we were gathered. He looked at us and said, "I can't believe what I am seeing right now. I recruited every one of you and did I ever tell you that this was going to be easy? Because gentlemen if you think this is hard wait until you get out there, (his arm extended and his index finger pointing up as to reference outside) that's where it is hard." I can vividly recall that single moment in my life as if it happened yesterday. That was the moment that he wasn't our football coach, but our mentor, trying to prepare us for the real world. Little did I know then how important that moment in my life would be. He taught us about how hard it was going to be in the real world, and boy was he right. He wasn't just a great coach, he was a great man and a great human being but, more than anything he was a great 'life' teacher. The sad thing is he passed away much too early, may God rest his soul.

I would like to thank Rick Hartzell for making the drive from Rochester to Austin to meet my parents and me at our house to recruit me to Northern Iowa. (As a credit to my mom's awesome cooking, he shared with me once it was one of the best pork chop dinners he had ever eaten.) He was the one person that believed in me enough to take me out of my home town and open my eyes to the outside world. If it would not have been for him, I don't know where I would have wound up.

I want to thank my daughter, Megan, for making me realize that I have faults and I am not a perfect human being, but there is nothing that makes me more proud than to have her as my daughter.

I want to thank my stepson, Michael, for being my inspiration on a daily basis, reinforcing why it is so important to help young adults be prepared for the real world.

When I think of having a passion, like mine to prepare young adults for the real world (my wife would beg to differ on this, she thinks it's sports), there is one man that has taught me much through his constant demonstration of his love of basketball, especially the Final Four. Thank you to my best friend for life, Dr. Bob. To have a best friend that accepts me for who I am is an unbelievable feeling.

I would also like to thank Jeanette and Jim DePhillips for their constant encouragement and support, believing in this endeavor and always pushing me forward. Your hospitality and generosity, early on, during my speaking engagements was wonderful and comforting.

Many thanks to my good friend, Rich Singer, for his careful eye and red pen.

Thanks, too, to Cory and Kristen Grosser for their unwavering support and an outstanding cover design.

To John Santos, for his constant encouragement and support but most of all his friendship. His passion for making a difference in the lives of young adults is an inspiration to me.

I would like to thank Michelle Bennett, to whom I owe so much for all the advice and wisdom she gave me, in addition to being one of the nicest people I have ever met. Thanks Michelle.

I would like to thank Mike Auer for the valuable advice on how important research information would be in my life.

I would also like to thank Dee and all of her staff at the Vermont Avenue Starbucks in Los Angeles for all those days that they allowed me to sit and work on this project; thanks for your support.

Thanks to all of my fellow Woodcraft Rangers, you know who you are, for all of your support and for listening to me share my trials and tribulations.

The words, last but not least, do not even begin to describe the feelings that I have for the most important person in my life and without her, none of this would be possible. I remember when I met her for the very first time, there was something about her that was very special but I just couldn't put my finger on it. As time went on and the more we worked together, we began to develop a friendship, having numerous conversations about every subject two people could discuss. Then there were the countless events that we worked on together, the days, the nights, the weekends, the book fairs, the street fairs, the auctions accompanied by the endless amounts of laughter and some tears (enough one time that she closed a restaurant, no kidding) but more than anything else a friendship like I have never experienced in my life, ever. She was there for me when I made the decision to stand up for myself, which became the launching point for me to follow my passion and move ahead in my life. She was the one who encouraged me to do whatever I needed to do, just as long as the journey was along the path to my ultimate happiness. All of her love and devotion, all of her pep talks, her belief in me is what has single-handedly turned my life around and has made it absolutely wonderful. To be able to have that one person with whom you share so much in common is an unbelievable feeling. The woman I need to thank more than anyone in my life is my wife, Ann. If there was ever a guardian angel that was dropped down from heaven to be with me as my soul mate, it was her. Thank you, honey, for all you have done for me.

ABOUT THE AUTHOR

Michael Wagner has over 25 years of professional work experience in the fields of finance, education, ethics and character education. Working in the independent and public school environment in Los Angeles, he discovered his passion to make a difference in the lives of young adults by helping them develop real life skills. He holds a Bachelors Degree in Administrative Management from the University of Northern Iowa and a Masters Degree in Educational Administration from the Michael D. Eisner School of Education at California State University – Northridge. Mike lives in Los Angeles with his wife, Ann and stepson, Michael, and has a 22 year old daughter, Megan.

Made in the USA
Lexington, KY
20 August 2014